Musings
of a
Thelemite

Musings
of a
Thelemite

Frater Da'Neos

Alchemy Press
Wright City, MO

www.alchemypress.org

Alchemy Press, Inc. Wright City, 63390
www.alchemypress.org
Published 2006. Printed in New York.
ISBN 0-9776911-0-1

For Katherine,

Who has ever supported me when I had no place to stand, ever believed in me when I had no faith in myself, for always pushing me on when I was ready to give up. You are my wife, my helpmate, my consort, my partner, and the feminine half of my soul. You make me BELIEVE.

For that, I will always love you.

Contents

Acknowledgments

I would like to thank the following people for believing in me and helping me in various ways with advice and friendship during the long writing of this book:

My muse Katherine, to whom this book is dedicated.

Adam Borrego, for encouragement, text reading, criticism, friendship, and a good smack in the head when I "fly off the handle." Whenever times have been darkest, you have never failed to help me to carry on. You are my best friend and spiritual brother; you have helped me to write this book more than you may know.

Joshua Koester, for your friendship and brotherhood upon the crooked path of enlightenment. We have both traveled a hard path, sometimes with pain and despair. You have made that path less painful, and have often helped me to keep faith, to continue when I have lost all hope. You're also pretty good at Tekken- almost as good as me. You have my eternal gratitude.

My father, for helping me to not starve to death while pursuing literary and academic aspirations, as well as giving me encouragement to follow my dreams. I only wish to make you proud, dad.

My Mother, for giving me her own brand of "tough love" whenever life begins to beat me down. Also for giving me much needed practical advice. As she always said, I have no common sense.

My cousin Forrest Lenzing, for being a light in my times of darkness, and ever showing me the unconditional love that only family can, and for making me laugh.

My Brother Billy, for your support and belief in me, and for looking up to me even though I'm not sure I am the best example to live by.

My academic friends, for pushing me on to accomplish what I need to in life: John Han, Cordell Schulten, and Mary Bagley.

Author J.F. Bierlein, for your candid encouragement and advice.

Andrea Wood "Princess of Disks," for teaching the lessons of life, ethics, women, and ambition as well as many good conversations over coffee. You will always be my friend, come what may.

Marshall Mathers, for your music, which I listened to while writing much of this.

Aleister Crowley, who did what he could.

There are many others who have helped me along the way, which have passed out of my life. To "Shakespeare," at the Café for your encouragement, David "motorcycle man," for fixing my bike, the Angel in the van from my past, Jeff "Modesto" Easterwood for some good times, Curtis Cantrell, wherever you are, perhaps we will meet again in life. Trevor Davis, who was once my brother but whom fate has divided from me. Dean Klossner, for teaching me the way of Bushido. Jeff the cook, for teaching me how to live; Pete the horse trader for buying me drinks at the bar.

I would like to offer a very special thanks to all of those who never believed in me, who spit on me, called me lazy and a liar. Those who said I would never amount to anything, and tried to kick me down for selfish reasons. All of your blows have only made the fire burn hotter, and may you rest in hell.

Forward

Nothing is more pertinent in this modern age of a spiritually starved and blinded society than an emissary of the cosmic Will. Pneuma has been pushed aside for the apparent superiority of the materialistic, and has been hidden behind skepticism, empiricism, and existentialism. The messenger of the cosmos bears two very important responsibilities: first, he must act as a teacher to those who have no natural method towards the spirit, or who require assistance from outside; second, the emissary acts as a stabilizing force within the world, ensuring that the connection to spirit does not fade entirely.

Presented in this book are the writings of a man during a particular mystical/magical time of his life; a period in which active discovery and involvement in the antinomian worlds of order and chaos were of utmost importance to his spiritual growth. This book therefore represents a path, and a path only. The goal itself is not mentioned, yet implied. To define this goal takes away from it, however, certain clues may be given so that the intellectual mind, a necessity for human comprehension, may lend itself to a spiritual understanding. The goal involves an experiential and intuitional understanding, one not influenced by the rational mind, but only interpreted by it.

This is a manuscript concerning the true nature of Thelema, not the idiocy expounded by ignorant individuals and insignificant orders. Thelema as a mystical tradition concerns itself with intuitional experience and theory, however, it is a theory derived from one's direct investigation into that which he experiences mystically. It is easy enough to say, "Do what thou wilt," but how many Thelemites actually understand this maxim? Thelema is the individualistic experience within the universal; it is madness within intellectualism, and Dionysianism versus asceticism. Thelema is sanity and madness, intellect and art, and classical and romantic thought together to form a new entity. Thelema is active and requires action; it is fire and burns the unnecessary things from the path with fury and vigor leaving only a charred landscape in its path. Here however, within the ashy remains lies the seed of Truth, which can only be seen once one has been destroyed; an action only the individual himself may perform.

One might therefore ask, given the above, "What good is a book that describes not the goal but a portion of the path to it?" The answer is that those who wish to find the goal must do so himself; he may look to others for guidance, but must take his own action; this is exactly what the author had in mind when publishing. To describe a path leads one closer to the goal; to describe the goal leads one further from it. Therefore, the author offers signposts in the darkness, leaving a trail for those who wish to follow.

This book has been separated into two primary portions, though not denoted as such. The first section is an intellectual investigation into the nature of Thelema, the forces that has lead to Thelema, and some more important theories concerning the tradition. The reader must take note however, that even though the word 'intellectual' is used, that the main force behind the intellection is the influence of intuitional experience. One cannot speak of a thing that he does not understand. One may describe a thing intellectually but cannot tell of its essence without an experiential background. For example, what is water like? One may begin to describe its molecular properties and qualities, etc., but one only knows it when he drinks it, when he is immersed in it, i.e., when he experiences water itself. In this matter, the author provides, as he has lived and experienced that which is the heart of Thelema. The second portion of the book takes on a different approach, that of a complete surrendering of divisive thought to a realm of abstracts and chaotic musings.

Presented here then is what the title professes, the musings of a Thelemite; but one must keep in mind what exactly this entails. A man continuously evolves as long as he is under the influence of the transcendent; what he is today is not what he is tomorrow. This book, then, represents not a goal, but represents the seeking itself. Too many people in modern society seek immediate gratification, and the goal itself becomes the predominant prize, while the path to that goal becomes insubstantial. However, this faulty thinking leads one to a state of abyssal existence, and to some of the 'illnesses' mentioned by sages of the past. When reading this book, and when contemplating its message, the reader should bear this in mind, and try to shift his thought to a timeless state rather than one that is temporal, and therefore susceptible to folly.

Adam Borrego

February 20th, 2005

Introduction
The Search for Truth

Since the vagaries of my youth I have long felt a great fascination with both religion and the occult. I sensed that there were those who knew something that I didn't, that there were answers I should know. At that early age, I didn't distinguish greatly between what is called religion and that which is termed the occult. Of course I was told that one was good and the other evil, but what I desired was knowledge rather than morality.

I was brought up in a very Christian atmosphere; some of my earliest memories are of my father reading the bible to me each night before I went to sleep. Both of my parents were strong believers, and so I was raised as a Southern Baptist. I remember getting "saved" and baptized. Around the time I was seventeen, when my mind was coming into fruition, I realized then that the only thing worth doing was of a spiritual nature. I myself had realized my mortality, and had a mid-life crisis. Most people are a little slower than I am and wait until half their life is actually over before figuring out that everything they are doing is pointless; luckily for myself I realized the fact at a young age, although I was still very much in the dark as to what to do about it.

At that time, my search into religion and spirituality was severely limited. I had grown up reading the Bible, but I remember feeling that the book hinted at much more. I looked into other sources, but the only "occult" things I had read was New Age effluvium that insulted my intelligence as the sort of cheap hackwork written by people more ignorant than I was. So I suppose that I became a Christian by default. Once I accepted this as my spiritual path, I cast aside all other concerns. I had become quite puritanical by the time I was eighteen. I gave up pork, and held long fasts, and every Sunday I prayed for eight hours.

Introduction

Somehow I managed to get myself married. I spent my honeymoon preparing for college to study for the ministry. I gave up tobacco and alcohol and any other vices I could detect in myself. It wasn't long before I felt the lack of discipline in the church in which I had grown up in. I remember feeling like a Templar at a social. At times I considered joining a monastery, but thought it would be a greater sin to abandon my wife. I disagreed on points of theology with Catholicism, but I admired the virtue and simplicity of the monks. I was a complete literalist when it came to the Bible, and I noticed that a number of other Christians were very lax in following the letter of the law. I searched in vain for a church that could live up to my standards. Finding nothing but chaff, I vowed to start my own church.

I started my church when I was nineteen years old. I was working as a cook and going to school, somehow I still found time for it. As I have said, I had the mentality of a Templar, and in many ways I still do. I called my church The Followers of Christ and began speaking to as many people as I could. Within a few months I had thirty or more people showing up and I couldn't fit any more. All this time I had been doing my best to study Hebrew and Greek Koine in order to read the Bible in direct translation. I was hungry for truth. I wanted to be a saint and become a sword of God.

Ironically, it was not temptation, but my zeal that broke me. I was digging further and further into the original texts when I began to notice contradiction and intentional mistranslations. I think I was around twenty at this time. In the contemporary Christian books I read, I saw weak, struggling arguments to fight off those intellectuals who saw the holes in the armor of Christ. It was these weak, pathetic lies that others were using to defend Christianity that first planted the seed of doubt, as I have always had a strong tendency to be brutally honest, seeing a liar as the ultimate coward.

I struggled with the issue for some time, but as I sought answers to the questions of faith that I had, instead of

being strengthened, I found only more reasons to doubt.
Finally one day I threw my bible on the floor and told
Jehovah to go to hell. Even during this time I was still
running my church. I felt like a total hypocrite, teaching
things that I didn't believe in. But they didn't know about
my spiritual downfall, I had kept that my little secret. My
loss of faith had plunged me into the darkest depression of
my life. This force that I had always depended on and
believed in suddenly wasn't there.

I remember thinking that it was much like when I
was younger and realized that Santa Claus didn't exist.
When I found out that old Saint Nick was a fraud, I was
crushed. I guess most children are upset, but for me it sent
my young six-year-old mind into premature nihilism. At
that moment I knew that if I had been fooled about Santa,
something that I had been so sure about, then perhaps all the
other things that I believed in were lies as well. So, lying
there in bed with tears in my eyes, I checked off the list of
things that must also be imaginary: tooth fairy, Easter
bunny, my imaginary friend, and God. Of course I later
recanted on the last one, but as I sat there looking down at
my mangled bible on the floor, I realized that I had been
right the first time.

I tried my best to break up the church on some
pretense. I remember that I didn't want to bring the others
down with me; I didn't want them to lose their faith because
I saw that it gave them joy, whereas I was in absolute
misery. Believing that ignorance is bliss, I hid the fact that I
was a heathen from everyone: my parents, my friends, and
my wife. This may seem to be in conflict with my statement
on honesty, but one must understand that being in the state
of despair I was in, I thought of nothing as bad as bringing
others into it. I began to return things that I had given up:
eating pork, drinking, watching porn.

Surprisingly my wife stayed as puritanical as ever.
She constantly rebuked me just as I had always done to
others. She threw words at me that she had heard from my
own mouth. Often women do not marry a man but an idea.

16

Introduction

Amid all the tumultuousness of my situation, I had to laugh at the irony of being chided by my own creation. As she kept to her beliefs, I slid into a cold logical atheism, hating myself for it at the same time. I developed a morbid fear of death once I was no longer sure of an afterlife. I became an absolute skeptic. I tried to interest myself in other forms of spirituality, but they always required faith, a faith I no longer had in anything and did not have the energy to summon.

Sometime when I was twenty years old I discovered Kabbala. This offered some peace between the wife and me. She had relaxed her standards somewhat, and she was happy that I was dealing with something that had a connection to Jehovah. I felt disgusted by anything mentioning prayer or faith, what I was really interested in was the tree of life. I realized this was something that might fill the spiritual nihilism of my soul, but it didn't require me to be "religious." Slowly the Kabbala pulled me in deeper and deeper, and I began to feel some of the old whisperings of my soul again.

It was during this time when I was once again on the road to understanding my place in life that the conflicts between my wife and me began anew. Although nominally still a Christian, her ways had slowly been changing. My lack of leadership in this area allowed her to be lax in her beliefs, and she never could accept my new ones. Its funny how many people are completely immobile in their thoughts. She was becoming disgusted with my lack of interest in material things, my lack of ambition to beg for position among people that I despised. Even though I had given up my Christian faith, never did I forget the truth that I had learned when I was seventeen: that if there is anything worthwhile, it is of a spiritual nature. So during the times that I lacked a deep spirituality, I simply didn't see anything at all worthwhile.

My wife saw things differently. She was a creature of the flesh. She wanted what this world had to offer those willing to beg and prostitute themselves for it. So she committed an unforgivable sin and betrayed me. She began having an affair with another man who she later ran off with. She haughtily told me how this guy could give her what she wanted. I told her that she would suffer tenfold for what she had done, but not by my hand. And I was absolutely correct, down to the last letter, but that is a whole other story.

Shortly after our break-up I met the Scarlet Woman,[1] who has been with me ever since. And unlike my ex-wife, who improperly tried to force her will upon my own, the Scarlet Woman understands the destiny that I have in accordance with my True Will, and my Will is her Will.

It was not long after I met the Scarlet Woman that I discovered Thelema. After we got together, I had continued to study Kabbala and Hermetic magick. I still went to school but I eventually switched my major from Theology to History to Computer Science to Philosophy and finally to English literature. The Scarlet Woman came to me at first as a student, saying that she wanted to learn magick. She had been reading some Wiccan garbage that I told her to throw out and commenced teaching her something about the nature of the esoteric. I had heard references to Aleister Crowley as a man who knew a great deal about Kabbala and so I went to the bookstore in order to find something by him. The store I went to had only one book of his: *The Gems of the Equinox*.

Crowley hit me like a tidal wave. I can honestly say that he did not so much shape my thinking, but rather supported and helped me to expand my views. As Robert Pirsig wrote, "When you live in the shadow of insanity, the appearance of another mind that thinks and talks as yours does is something close to a blessed event. Like Robinson Crusoe's discovery of footprints on the sand."[2] Contained within this book, among a great deal of other things, was

---

[1] For all those who wish to jump up in arms on my use of this term, I might add that I am not implying that she is *the* scarlet woman, merely *my* scarlet woman. Those who have too many shackles on their brain to understand this can go to hell.
[2] Pirsig, *Zen*, 233.

Introduction

The Book of the Law. I devoured everything I could find by Crowley after that, amazed to find another man who was staring at the same monument, albeit from a different location. Crowley is perhaps one of the most unrecognized geniuses of the twentieth century. The only men who can compare to his mind are all hailed as giants of the intellectual world. Not only is he the foremost writer on scientific illuminism, but also a substantial linguist, poet, philosopher, and sociologist who has influenced our society more than many realize. Since that time I have spent a great deal of time studying and meditating on the three short chapters of the Book of the Law, and on that great corpus of work that Frater Perdurabo has left behind. It was not until much later that I read *The Law is for All*, which includes part of Crowley's commentary. By the time I read Crowley's commentary I had already formed a good understanding concerning the nature of the book and was pleased to find Crowley's views to be in agreement with and an expansion of my own.

After I had become a student of the Kabbala, and later as a Thelemite, I often hated the fact that I had wasted years of my life in service to Christianity. Not only was it a sore point for my ego, but I also felt that time which could have been spent on the Great Work was thrown away to a farce. But now I realize it isn't so. I have gained a very deep understanding of the Christian religion, far deeper in fact than 97.23% of Christians themselves. Not only the insight of the scholar, which could be dismissed. But being so driven by the religion, being such a zealot, I understand very deeply what it is that makes the whole religion, and consequently the followers of that religion. I have come to realize also that it has given me insight into the Aeon of Osiris, which in turn has given me a much deeper understanding and appreciation of the Aeon of Horus.

In all of my studies I suppose it can be said that I have learnt a number of "truths." In putting this book together I have tried as best as able to avoid repetition of things already said elsewhere. Alas, some overlapping is inevitable, and I have found that if a person wishes to restrict himself to writing only that which is completely original, then he will write nothing at all. So in my search for truth, I have tried to find that which is most pure and look at it in terms of what others have said. All of this is done in a Thelemic/Hermetic/Gnostic mindset. Of course in any search one could do worse than following the maxim of Andre Gide, "Believe those who are seeking the truth. Doubt those who find it." In that context I would like to say that I am not presenting something I expect others to follow like scripture, in fact I don't recommend even following scripture in that way. As the title indicates, these are musings, and as such can be taken as serious or farcical as one pleases.

In many ways I am conflicted in even writing a book. I think that writing is the most presumptuous thing that anyone can ever do. The entire process rests on the idea that other people will pay to read your scribbles. In many cases the writers have been vindicated by the populace, but more often than not they are ridiculed for their presumption that anyone would be interested in such drivel. Samuel Johnson is attributed to saying, upon looking at one man's work, "Your manuscript is both good and original, but the part that is good is not original and the part that is original is not good."

If the reader finds himself or herself confused by what is presented here, then they are not alone. I barely know what I am talking about myself. I find it is difficult enough to announce what I think without having to remember why it is I think it. In many cases I begin an essay, and then when I am part way through with it, find that I have taken the exact opposite opinion. Or else I am going along and writing, only to find that it is at odds with what I had written in a different essay. I think that is why I made such a poor minister: I am not very good at telling people what to think, at least not with any sort of consistency. But perhaps it might just be that a person will look at the various warping, non-consistent scrawling and gain from it. I certainly think that it is of greater edification than picking at

20

a scab, but perhaps my critics will prove me wrong. If that indeed happens to be the case, I shouldn't be very much bothered, for as Emerson has said, "What I must do is all that concerns me, not what the people think."[3] By the time I actually have a published copy of this book I will most likely disagree with some of what I have wrote. I find that I must be continually evolving, ever changing in a cyclic motion, to drink of new things in life. You cannot taste of the same river twice.

    With all of that in mind, the reader might likely ask, "then why do you write?" That is a very appropriate question, and as soon as I figure out the answer to that I will write it down. Of course, I did have an answer to that question just yesterday, but as I no longer believe it to be true, I will not transcribe it here. I suppose I could say it is my True Will, but that answer is put forth so often that I think it is starting to sound lame. I write because I do, and why be damned. At least I have Emerson to come to my defense, in his essay "Self-Reliance":

> A foolish consistency is the hobgoblin of little minds, adored by little statesmen and philosophers and divines. With consistency a great soul has simply nothing to do. He may as well concern himself with his shadow on the wall. Speak what you think now in hard words and to-morrow speak what to-morrow thinks in hard words again, though it contradict every thing you said to-day. – 'Ah, so you shall be sure to be misunderstood.' – Is it so bad then to be misunderstood? Pythagoras was misunderstood, and Socrates, and Jesus, and Luther, and Copernicus, and Galileo, and Newton, and every pure and wise spirit that ever took flesh. To be great is to be misunderstood.[4]

---

[3] *The Portable Emerson*, 143.
[4] Ibid., 145-46.

Musings of a Thelemite

In my life I have never really been satisfied with any religion. I have bounced around through the whole gamut, taking little bits and running as soon as they try to impose rules or order on me. Generally I take what I like. This is true of me as concerns Thelema as well. As of this very moment, I cannot say that I am overly dogmatic about Thelema, or the prophecies of Crowley. I use it principally as a paradigm, as I find it fits my needs much better than any other system I have seen. Any system, including Thelema, is a two-edged sword. It can be used to free your mind, and it can be used to enslave it. Which happens is totally determined by your will. That being said, I do not look at Crowley as the pope of Thelema, nor do not find him to be infallible.

One thing that I have become fairly sure of is that attempts to categorize that which lies beyond us can be no more than that: attempts. In this sense, it is not more correct to call "that which is beyond" an image upon the subconscious, than it is to call it an angel or what not. It is beyond human comprehension, but not beyond human experience. There is something there. Thousands of years and millions of people attest to this. For those that see others dipping into this gnosis, they require "faith." For the Gnostic himself, he needs nothing. When the Gnostic element leaves or steps out of a system, or is forbidden by legalism, then that religion becomes codified into rules based on one Gnostic's experiences. Unfortunately, this is what many would see done with the system of Thelema.

It is similar to the testing of rats. Sometimes one will spin around before pushing a button that deposits the food. Thus he thinks that it is necessary. So if a Gnostic shaved his head, or abstained from eating eggs, then it becomes a rule of the religion. For, by applying "reason," and cause and effect, they believe that such things will get them where the Gnostic was. Jonathon Swift commented on this fact in *Gulliver's Travels*, writing:

> Difference in opinions hath cost many millions of lives; for instance, whether the juice of a certain berry be blood or wine; whether whistling be a

Introduction

vice or a virtue; whether it be better to kiss a post, or throw it into the fire; what is the best color for a coat, whether black, white, red, or grey; and whether it should be long or short, narrow or wide, dirty or clean; with many more. Neither are any wars so furious and bloody, or of so long continuance, as those occasioned by difference in opinion, especially if it be in things indifferent.[5]

Here is made a snide reference to the various theological debates that were ongoing, and which did in fact cost many lives. Buddha, Mohammad, and Jesus all proclaimed teachings for the world, and none of them seem to agree with one another with regards of right and wrong. But there is something unmistakable in each of them, and that is the fact that each of them acquired their genius through sheer will. I realize this is not a new point, as Crowley admirably dealt with this subject in various places. I only ask that it be remembered, even when dealing with Thelema, that the only sin is restriction. As Harold Bloom remarked, "Seeking God outside the self courts the disasters of dogma, institutional corruption, historical malfeasance, and cruelty."[6]

Far better than these rules are other forms of non-rationalistic religious experience, which is often rejected in the western religions, i.e. art, music, sex, and drugs. These are the catalyst for the non-Gnostic who cannot, at least at first, find God within. But these "mystical experiences" should not be confused to be equivalent to, nor equal as the true mystical awareness that comes with no aid other than oneself. These former experiences are far inferior, and although in some cases are helpful, in many other do more harm than good. Bloom, in a conversation with one of his students, remarked, "The sorrow of the Anesthetic Revelation is that the music stops, the drug wears off, and there is no spiritual aftermath, or at least no awareness that

---

[5] Swift. *Gulliver's Travels*, 2442.
[6] Harold Bloom. *Omens of Millennium*, 14.

can be put into words. That however is preferable to New Age prose, which is of a vacuity not to be believed."[7]

It could be argued that had Crowley not played with drugs, he would have been able to accomplish much more in his later years, and suffered far less in his health. That is not an attack on Crowley, as the nature and danger of cocaine, heroin, and opium was not fully understood at that time, and Crowley thought that all drugs were equal in terms of setting them aside. I can imagine the shame he must have felt upon becoming hopelessly addicted, after proclaiming in many places that addiction was only for the weak-willed. In this case, Crowley's pride and ego were his downfall. Since he is the first and greatest teacher of Thelema, let us learn from his life, and the mistakes that he made rather than pursuing blind imitation. Neither being an ego-slave or chemical dependency will get you very far.

I am anti-empiricist when it comes to religion and truth. Gnosis is not perspectivism per se. It is explained in personal perspectives, but this Gnosis is Truth. Hence, truth is not logical. Gnosis is deeper than logic. Religious experience cannot be measured or judged rationally. Nor can it be understood psychologically, as gnosis is deeper than mind or psychology. Thus we have the oft-repeated phrase: "Every word spoken is a lie."

This phrase was often repeated by Crowley himself. The clever boy will ask the teacher, "So does this mean that the words spoken to Crowley on April 8th, 9th, and 10th, in 1904 were lies?" In one sense it must be admitted that they were, as language is incapable of transmitting pure truth. Language is a prison, and it corrupts everything. But of course, things are not as black and white as all of that. There are degrees of truth, so that in one sense, some things are more valuable than others. Of course, from this also comes the concept that nothing is completely without value, no matter how untrue it is. I think dogmatism slows down many Thelemites, who argue about the capitalization of

---

[7] Ibid., 19.

Introduction

certain letters, or where a period should be, whether things should be done this way or that, and so on. It is indeed ironic that there are "fundamentalist" Thelemites, a term that really should be oxymoronic.

The Three Aeons

**The time has come when we have to pay for having been
Christians for two thousand years. – Friedrich Nietzsche**

What do the Aeons really signify? The phrase,
"Aeon of Horus" is repeated often enough, and sometimes is
partially explained, but what does it mean in the larger sense
of things? I believe that we actually have passed through at
least three Aeons, and that these periods can be identified by
certain characteristics. Of course, this Thelemic division into
Aeons is not the only way into which history can be
esoterically divided. Among other systems, I think that the
astrological method is particularly thought provoking. But
as I am not very educated on astrology, I will leave that to
those who are.

When studying the Aeons of Thelema, or any
divisions of human history, the greatest tools from which to
perceive the times of the past are mythology and
anthropology. I think that in the main, mythology is short
changed and its real value is left buried. As some have said,
mythology is nothing more than a religion no one believes in
anymore. By this definition, there are truly few myths left
nowadays and many religions; the worship of Egyptian,
Norse, and Greek deities has been rekindled, as well as
many others. Whether or not this modern day worship
resembles anything like the original religions is open to
debate, and in any case it may not matter.

The Hindus say that there is "one God, but he goes
by many names." In the same fashion, all the many deities
can be said to be aspects of the One. This was true in many
religions, even in ancient times. Those polytheists often
understood that there was one deity above all, who was so
great that he was unapproachable. The much-vaunted
monotheism of Christianity replaced these lesser deities with
archangels and saints early on, as the populace needed
something it could interact with.

The Three Aeons

There is no religion in the world, now or in the past, that is pure and without the influence of other belief systems. Every religion is a culmination of various factors that were building previously. Any time two or more religions existed at the same time, they influenced and changed one another, even if these systems of belief were mortal enemies. Thus, Zoroastrianism influenced Judaism and Christianity; Christianity influenced Mohammedanism, and so on until it becomes difficult to determine where certain superstitions or doctrines came from originally.

In many cases a religion began as a reaction to a different religion. This is the case with Babylonian religion reacting against the cult of Tiamat, Judaism reacting against the Babylonian theology, Christianity reacting against Judaism then Gnosticism, Mohammedanism reacting against Christianity, and finally by Gnosticism being absorbed into all these religions, yet also persisting as a separate entity as well. It is Gnosticism that is the most fluid of the beliefs to follow, especially since it never bothered to establish itself as an organized religion. Of course, after all of that, we have Thelema as a reaction against Christianity, Judaism, Mohammedanism, Hinduism, Buddhism, and anything else you wish to throw in. But its special enemy always seems to be Christianity.

Practically everything in Thelema is an affront to the Christian belief system. From its prophet, "The Beast 666" and his Scarlet Woman, to Liber V, the "mark of the beast." There are many parallels from *The Book of the Law* to the Book of Revelation in the Bible. It must be surmised that the Aeon of Horus fulfilled the prophecies of that book, (albeit in a manner that Christians were never expecting) that Crowley purposely used such terminology in the book to attack Christianity, or that such a flavor was the inevitable unconscious result of Crowley's harsh upbringing. I leave it as an open question.

The Aeon of Isis

In the earliest of times, worship was centered on the great earth mother. In those times, it was seen that humanity had sprung from the earth. Worship often centered in caves, which were seen to be the womb of the great mother. All plant life seemed to spring miraculously from the soil, which provided life. The human female seemed to be deeply connected with these mysteries, whose monthly cycle of blood coincided with the moon. When woman gave birth, then her body produced food like the earth in the form of milk. Woman and the goddess were seen to be the sources of all life.

Joseph Campbell has shed a great deal of light on this era in his book, *Occidental Mythology*. According to him, the earliest period of the mother goddess cult was perhaps between c. 7500-3500 B.C. During this time she was most likely viewed in simple terms of fertility, but even by 3500 B.C. she had become of much more importance. She represented the potency of time, space, and all matter; she was the force of life and death, which at this time was not opposed in duality but united and understood to be twin aspects of the same concept. There was no concept that was outside of her, everything that could be conceived of resided in her womb.[8]

---

[8] Campbell, *Occidental Mythology*, 7.

The Great Mother

The great mother provided sustenance but was also cold and cruel. By giving life she also condemned us all to death. She seemed to bring life out of instinct rather than out of any sort of love: she was perfectly content letting the forces of nature rack and ail us, letting only the fit survive. It was the great mother who caused the will to death, the call to rest and peace, the opening of the eye of Shiva. To live in her world was for life to be harsh, short, and brutal. Her primary concern was with procreation for the advancement of biological evolution. After we have proven ourselves fit to survive (thus passing her test) and have produced offspring (thus performing her work) she is finished with the experiment and calls us back. She does not protect the weak, considering them to be failures. In many ways she is cold and indifferent, an unconscious force.

She was "darkly ominous," and appeared sometimes as a singular goddess, but often enough as multiples. She was "the mother of both the living and the

dead," and her consort was typically a serpent, but
sometimes a dove. Her rites were not bright with "manly
athletic games" of the later eras. Her worship was far away
from the magnanimous worship of the later male deities,
which was accompanied by "humanistic art, social
enjoyment, feasting and theater." The mother goddess was
dark and primitive; further away from civilization, indeed
the force of nature herself, which all too often gets painted
while wearing rose-tinted glasses. She was nature in all its
heartless cruelty. The lion that tears the gazelle's flesh, the
gasping, rotting corpses of diseased bodies: all this is the
true earth mother. Those who most often mourn the loss of
the old mother's rites are ignorant of what they truly were.
They were conducted with a "spirit dark and full of dread.
The offerings were not of cattle, gracefully garlanded, but of
pigs and human beings; directed downward, not upward to
the light; and rendered not in polished marble temples,
radiant at the hour of rosy-fingered dawn, but in twilight
groves and fields, over trenches through which the fresh
blood poured into the bottomless abyss."[9]

There is also a remarkable aspect of the old mother
worship that is particularly of interest to the hermetic
practitioner. During the rites, there was always the concept
"that if the negative aspect of the daemon were dispelled,
health and well-being, fertility and fruit, would issue of
themselves from their natural source."[10] Which to be
interpreted, means that the rites were always either of
banishment and appeasement. The mother's brood, which
might be likened to an immense multitude of non-civilized,
non-rational demons, had to be gotten rid of. If this were
done, then the people would benefit. This is strictly a
negative ritual. It is in marked contrast to the later rituals of
the sun gods, which were of invocation. The sun god did not
have to be appeased in order to exist; rather one could

---

[9] Ibid., 17.
[10] Ibid., 18.

simply live better with the sun god's blessings, and with his force residing within.

It is important however to not view either the sun god or the earth mother as objectively good or bad. What is now considered abhorrent at one time was considered holy and vice versa. Throughout all of these Aeons it must be remembered that there is an evolution of consciousness occurring, and to the people who were living in a particular time, they were doing what was morally right.

An interesting sub-point in morals was the custom in India of burning the wives of men on the funeral pyre with them. The practice was started due to the habit of wives killing their husbands, so that they might inherit his money without having anyone to tell them what to do. After the funeral practices were started, it might be surmised that this particular habit of wives decreased rapidly. This practice was forbidden as uncivilized by Great Britain after it gained dominion over India; at which point the murder rate of men spiked once again.

The Serpent

During this era of development, there was no father god per se. There were male deities to be sure, the serpent deity being the most important at this time, but they were all under the great mother, and their authority was in virtue of their relationship to the mother, whether in the form of consort, son, or both. In the later age of Osiris, many of these original connections would be reversed. So, for instance, in ancient myth the snake was the lover of the goddess, but in the Book of Genesis, where Eve is a stand-in for the mother, the snake is transformed into a thing of evil.[11]

It is important not to view the serpent of Genesis as a devil, Satan, et cetera, for this was a much later modification, not by the Hebrews but the Christians, who sought to further defame the majesty of the serpent. They later made their Satan horned and goat-hoofed in order to

---

[11] Ibid., 9.

attack the followers of Pan. It is nothing more than religious propaganda against what presents a deep and complex, therefore competing, understanding of spirituality. It is what Campbell terms "mythic defamation" by making the gods of other peoples the demons of one's own mythology, while at the same time "enlarging one's own counterparts to hegemony over the universe." A series of lesser myths is then created to show how one's deity is supreme over the lesser deity. One marked example of this is with the plagues upon Egypt by the hand of Moses, which were actually directed at the chief deities of the sun, Nile, et cetera. The chief purpose is to "validate in mythological terms not only a new social order but also a new psychology."[12] So in this sense the alteration of myth can actually move human consciousness forward, by breaking ties with the past. This is the case where the solar deity replaced the earth mother. But in the case of Christianity and Pan we cannot be so congenial, for it was not superseding the old mythology in this case, but attempting to shadow out a fellow solar deity, as properly understood.[13]

In the case of Thelema, a mythical reinterpretation occurred as pertains to the Book of Revelation. Previously, the events described in the book were taken to be a literal event that would mark the end of the world, with fire and death. The Great Beast would rise, and only those who took the mark of the beast would be able to buy or sell. This came to have a different interpretation under the Law of Thelema. The fire and death came certainly, and is still coming. For those who accept The Book of the Law, the Great Beast has risen in the person of TO MEGA THERION. And it could be said that those who do not have the mark of the beast, either in the form of Liber V vel Reguli, or by acceptance of the Law of Horus, has no spiritual currency, as all the old ways have perished.

---

[12] Ibid., 80.
[13] Vide infra, Mythological Defamation of Pan

The Three Aeons

This mythical defamation in the Aeon of Osiris only occurred with what later became known as the "orthodox" Christians, which is a product of Pauline Christianity. For the early Gnostic Christians, who were in many ways a more original breed of Christianity, the serpent remained one of their most holy figures and symbols, which they equated with Christ as a bringer of knowledge and as one who releases one from oppression. To the Gnostic, both Jesus and the serpent were a counterforce to the evil of Jehovah or the demiurge, and coins of the era depict a crucified Jesus on one side, and a serpent mounting the cross upon the other. The Naassene Gnostics had a hymn that ended "All hail, all hail –as Pan, as Bacchus, as shepherd of the shining stars." Their name itself comes from the Hebrew word *nahash*, "serpent."[14] So when I refer to Christians, it must be understood that I refer to the heirs of the Roman church and not the early Gnostic Christians.

To realize the magnitude of the reversal of the serpent, it must be understood that the serpent deity had been venerated for seven thousand years before the composition of Genesis. One notable manifestation of this serpent deity was the Sumerian Ningizzida, who was "Lord of the Tree of Truth." His image was often shown in the form of two mating vipers twisted about a staff in way very similar to the caduceus.[15] Despite the claims of later Yahwehist priests, the serpent continued to be worshipped by people of the Levant, including the Hebrews. Moses fashioned a staff of Ningizzida when the people were afraid of the serpents, thus giving one demonstration of what is to be shown again and again: that the Hebrew people were not a monotheistic race, until much later when the Levite priests codified the temple cult around 400 B.C. Even then, the official religion of the priests often conflicted with the will of the people. That is why the Old Testament is full of prophets, telling people to return to the god of their fathers,

---

[14] Barnstone and Meyer, *The Gnostic Bible*, 482-83.
[15] Campbell, *Occidental Mythology*, 9.

and to tear down the "high places" which were in effect poles dedicated to various gods, similar in form and function to the totem poles of the Native Americans.

Returning to the nature of the serpent deity, one of his most interesting aspects is his non-duality. That he is a phallic symbol is obvious, but the serpent is also a swallower, thus making him a symbol of the female as well.[16] In fact, I would go so far as to say that the serpent, as we now understand it, could be equated with the symbol of the ying-yang. But even in this powerful symbol, there is separateness, a duality that had not even been conceptualized at this point. To those of the mother goddess there was only unity.

Interestingly, the feminine concept of spirituality was later crushed in the West but continued in the East. It reached its full development in the religions of Buddhism, Hinduism, and Taoism. India is an interesting case, as it was close enough to the west to receive the male hero influences, but being historically perhaps the most religiously tolerant culture, they have even now evidence of both matriarchal and patriarchal practices, which may be seen in Tantra and Yoga, respectively. What is very interesting is that within the Indian mythology we have Shiva the Destroyer, who is a male deity. But his symbols are the crescent moon, the serpent, and the cow; also is he considered having dominion over the sea and is sometimes depicted as holding a trident. In Shiva's true form, he is neither male nor female, and thus beyond all dualities, which is the apex of earth mother theology.

It is also to be pointed out that Thelema is neither patriarchal nor matriarchal but puerarchal, being the glory of the child and honoring both mother and father. Thus we have the great mother in Nuit, her snake consort in Hadit, and the child of them in Ra-Hoor-Khuit; which is covered in depth below.

---

[16] Ibid., 10.

The Aeon of Osiris

The mentality of the patriarchal tribes can best be summed up by the words of Marduk to his father, Ea:

> His fear was gone. "I will accomplish," said the Lord Marduk, "all that is in your heart. Tiamat, a woman, is coming at you with arms. Soon you will trample on her neck. But O Lord of the destiny of the great gods, if I am to be your avenger, to slay Tiamat and keep you alive, convene the assembly and proclaim my lot supreme, namely, that not you but I shall henceforth fix the destinies of the gods by utterances and that whatever I create shall remain without change."[17]

With thus words was the Aeon of Osiris brought in. The old mother was now seen as a nuisance, a mother of a swarm, and the time of the Hero was born. In this era, the idea of the communal spirit has been suppressed in order for individuals to flourish. The will and mind of the Hero, the father slays the old mother and establishes his dominancy. In the case of the Greeks, the battle is shown in Zeus's defeat of Gaea's child Typhon, when he "sprang from his mountain and, hurling the bolt, set fire to all those flashing, bellowing, roaring, baying, hissing heads," which secured the dominancy of the patriarchal gods "over the earlier Titan broods of the great goddess mother." This theme is repeated again with Indra's defeat of the great serpent Vritra in the Vedic myths.[18] This idea is recurring in many traditions and is a very important turning point.

Man, through rational individualism and self-awareness, had overcome the mother in some extent. This is the male instinct of independence as opposed to the unconscious community of the mother and nature. That is why individualism is the male force and community is the female force. The male star develops from the center

---

[17] Ibid., 81.
[18] Ibid., 22-23.

outward and the female star develops from the outside inwards. The male is the force of creation, the female of assimilation. The self-awareness of the female is the spark of male force, which is not as strong as the unconscious and instinct in woman. In male, the spark is stronger, thus weakening the unconscious, and setting every male star in opposition to the great mother. When the male consciousness gained independence from the mother by becoming fully self-aware, then the Aeon of Osiris began.

But although separate, the great mother still overshadowed the male spark, looming above it. Thus was the continual action of self-sacrifice, which was an illusion of self-will. An illusion I say, because although the male spark appears to be independent, he really lets himself be returned to the great mother willingly, and does so on the premise of benefiting the community. Thus we have the soft effeminate Jesus, who was dragged back into the embrace of the great mother.

Campbell reveals that with the dawn of the Iron Age (c. 1250 BC) the old myths of the goddess were greatly altered and even suppressed by "those suddenly intrusive patriarchal warrior tribesmen whose traditions have come down to us chiefly in the Old and New Testaments and in the myths of Greece." There are two main sources of those who followed the male hero myths: the Semitic people of the Syro-Arabian deserts, and the Hellenic-Aryans from the plains of Europe and southern Russia. Before the invaders arrived, the world-view was "essentially organic, vegetal, non-heroic," which was "completely repugnant to those lion hearts for whom not the patient toil of earth but the battle spear and its plunder were the source of both wealth and joy."[19]

These patriarchal warrior tribesmen realized that woman did not produce life autonomously. She required the seed of man, without which she was totally barren. This gave new prestige and power to the concept of the father

[19] Ibid., 7, 21.

god. In addition, it was also understood by these tribes that the earth could not bring forth vegetation without the rays of Sol. Thus the sun became associated with the great father, and these societies linked their chief father deity with the sun and the sky, where the earth was the place of the mother.

The great mother's influence was greatly reduced when it became obvious that she depended on the sun's rays to give life. But the earth mother was not forgotten. This is quite evident in many cultures. In many cases there arose a fierce conflict between those who worshipped the earth mother in the old ways, and the new followers of the sun. As Campbell so aptly puts it, "No one familiar with the mythologies of the goddess of the primitive, ancient, and Oriental worlds can turn to the Bible without recognizing counterparts on every page."[20]

When people realized their all-dependence on the sun for life, then they began to fear darkness. Eclipses were seen as especially terrifying, for it was not known whether the sun god would return. Also the winter months were greatly feared, as the light of the sun became weaker and weaker. Thus was the winter solstice celebrated, with evergreen trees, which are now used as Christmas trees. Originally these were used in offering because of their greenness, to coax the sun back to summer. Thus was it realized that every year the sun died and then returned to life. The concept of the dying god was born. There are numerous examples of the death-rebirth mythos in various religions. These are much more familiar to us, because it was not long ago that we left that formula. The rites of Dionysus, Osiris, Christianity, and Mithraism all conform to the dying god concept within the Aeon of Osiris. Thus when Jesus died there was an eclipse, symbolizing the death of the sun.

---

[20] Ibid., 9.

Christianity

Out of the various religions that have developed within the last two thousand years, Christianity has had a greater effect on western civilization than any other. To view Christianity as the only representative of the Aeon of Osiris would be a mistake, as Buddhism, Zoroastrianism, and Mohammedanism, among others are perfect examples, although highlighting different aspects. But as it is likely that those who will read this book will have been exposed to Christianity more than any other, as indeed I was in my youth, so I will concentrate on it as an example.

Early Christian History: Jesus the Mystic

The historical reality of Jesus the man is somewhat doubtful, although it is a subject that continues to be debated by scholars. On this subject, Crowley remarked in his *Confessions*:

> The truth was that scraps of several such men, distinct from and incompatible with each other, had been pitch-forked together and labeled with a single name. It was exactly the case of the students who stuck together various parts of various insects and asked their professor, 'what kind of bug is this?' 'Gentlemen,' he replied, 'this is a humbug.'[21]

Crowley is not the only one to have advanced such a view. His position has been vindicated by succeeding scholarship. I am more of the mind, however, that there was a man named Jesus, who was a Jewish teacher. I think that this fish tale grew quite a bit out of proportion, however. One should always be weary of stories told by fishermen. The time was ripe for a new religion, and there had been a great welling of religious ideas at that time. There also existed at that time a sect of Jews called the Essenes, who may have had a great deal to do with the Messiah craze that had been building even before Jesus hit the scene.

---

[21] Crowley, *Confessions*, 809.

The Three Aeons

The Essenes

There were three primary sects of Jews during the time of Jesus: the Essenes, Pharisees, and Sadducees. They numbered about four thousand, and resided along the Dead Sea. They were the authors of the Dead Sea scrolls that were recently discovered. The Essenes originated around 150 B.C. and disappeared around the end of the first century A.D. As Jews, they worshiped one God, who was the creator of all things. They held Moses in high regard, and "to blaspheme his name meant death." They did not go to the temple in Jerusalem to sacrifice for fear of being polluted by others. They substituted gifts that they sent, and their pious lifestyle.[22]

They observed the Sabbath with such strictness that even the call of nature was refused. They were highly concerned with cleanliness and ritual bathing, and "even for a junior to touch a senior was pollution for the latter." They looked forward to death, as they viewed the flesh as corrupt and they longed for release. In some of their ways they appeared to be similar to the Gnostics. They rejected philosophy as uselessness, but paid careful attention to ethics. They were quite wise in many practical ways as well. They knew a great deal about medicinal remedies, and would heal others despite their religious beliefs. Apparently they also took to studying the properties of various minerals.[23]

One of the more interesting aspects of the Essenes is that they were, in both philosophy and practice, communists. They were forbidden to own anything personally, as a steward held every thing in common stock. Even their houses were shared by others as they willed. Even so, their contemporaries made remarkable reports of them. It was said that they lived to great age, and "they acquired such fortitude of mind and body that the worst

---

[22] Graham, *"Essenes."*
[23] Ibid.

torments inflicted on them by the Romans failed to shake their constancy and they met death with a smile."[24]

The Essenes were by and large men, and most of these rejected marriage. They did so not because they saw marriage as wrong, but rather did not trust women. They were a secretive bunch and feared the woman's gossiping nature. In addition to that, they desired peace and harmony more than anything. To keep the sect from dying out, they often adopted children. Their numbers were also maintained by converted outsiders who were made to go through a period of testing that lasted many years. When they were finally admitted as full members, they were made to swear "fearful oaths," promising "to conceal nothing from their fellows, and to reveal nothing to strangers." They viewed their book of angels as their greatest secret of all, which contained their various true names and attributions.[25]

Jesus the Apocalyptic Prophet

In looking at the beginnings of the religion, it was started by a man that is now called Jesus[26], who was a Jewish rabbi, opposed to the formalism that some showed toward Jewish law. He did not come to redeem the world; in fact he was only concerned with people of Jewish decent. When he sent his disciples out, he told them, "Go not into the way of the Gentiles, and into any city of the Samaritans enter ye not; but go rather to the lost sheep of the house of Israel."[27]

There were a great many in the first century who believed in this Jesus, expected his second coming, as Jesus himself had said:

> The sun shall be darkened, and the moon shall
> not giver her light. And the stars of heaven shall
> fall, and the powers that are in heaven shall be

---

[24] Ibid.
[25] Ibid.
[26] Let it not be supposed that I am in any way speaking of Jesus as a historical person, any more than Marduk slaying Tiamat was a historical event. All mythology, including Christianity, is based on certain historical events, but has been changed and enlarged to support the adherents of the myth in question.
[27] Holy Bible, Matthew 10:5-6

40

shaken. And then shall they see the Son of man coming in the clouds with great power and glory. And then shall he send his angels, and shall gather together his elect from the four winds, from the uttermost part of the earth to the uttermost part of heaven. [...] Verily I say unto you, that this generation shall not pass, till all these things be done.[28]

There has been no small amount of debate concerning this passage, and the meaning of the word "generation" here. The only way to settle questions of meaning is to go back to what original texts we have. In Greek, the word given here is *genea*, which primarily means generation as we use the word today: the lifetime of man, roughly sixty or eighty years. The word can be translated in other ways, however, and this is what biblical apologists use in defense. Secondary meanings of the word are age, nation, or time. The nation of Israel, although now reestablished, definitely passed away before the coming of the events described, if taken literally. As for the translation of *genea* as "age," I hardly think that we are in the same historical age as Jesus of Nazareth.

It could be further argued that all of those events were symbolic of other things, and that they did indeed occur before the end of that generation. This is the only view which might be acceptable, but I would dare say it would be difficult to find someone in a church today, either protestant or Catholic, who hold this view. The most common explanation is that here generation means "a people," and since there are still people of Hebrew descent living in the world today, then it is still possible for it to happen. There are two problems with this view however. Firstly, it would be the equivalent of telling someone that "this shall come to pass, before the oceans all evaporate." To give such a prophecy would be useless. The second reason that such a

---

[28] Holy Bible, Mark 13:24-30

view is preposterous is the actions of the Christians themselves.

Many of the early Christians sold their houses and all of their possessions, giving the money to the poor, as Jesus had commanded them. They then sat around, looking into heaven and awaiting his return at the head of his army of angels to free Jerusalem from the Romans. Ironically enough, his tardiness in returning estranged him from the Jews but eventually he was accepted by those very Romans who had conquered the Jews, who later took to terrorizing the Jews in the name of Jesus. But I get ahead of myself. The point is that these Christians weren't taking these words to be symbolic in the least.

After the people had been sitting around in the desert for about twenty years, and most if not all of the people who had actually known Jesus were already dead, a few bright fellows thought it might be a good idea to write some of it down before it was forgotten about all together. Of course, by this time, all sorts of other philosophies and religious beliefs had melded together with the original Jewish teaching. Many of the early Christians couldn't seem to agree on what Jesus actually said or did. The (somewhat) homogenous account as given in the New Testament today is the product of 2,000 years of careful editing.

The notable historian Frederick B. Artz has written: "No part of the New Testament seems to have been written by anyone who had ever seen Jesus or had heard him speak. The earliest book, in the form in which we have it, is probably St. Paul's first Epistle to the Thessalonians of about A.D. 50, and the last, the second Epistle of Peter of about A.D. 150."[29] As I have already stated, Jesus was a rabbi, or mystical teacher in the tradition of Judaism. His teachings were very simple and direct, as is illustrated by the Gospel of Thomas. Incidentally, this book was precluded from the authorized Bible when it was formed around 185 A.D. Jesus the man was of rather simple intentions and demeanor, and

---

[29] Artz, *Mind of the Middle Ages*, 53-54.

certainly unlearned. Artz concludes that "All the later, elaborate theories of original sin, of free will versus predestination, of the nature of the Trinity, of the Virgin Birth, and many other dogmas of the church would probably have amazed him."[30]

Christianity after Jesus

Paul

To give credit (or blame?) where it is due, the formation of Christianity, and its spread beyond the boarders of Israel was largely accomplished by one man, who never even met Jesus or read any Christian writings: St. Paul of Tarsus. Without him, the religion would almost certainly have puttered out by the end of the first century.[31] St. Paul did far more than the simple carpenter of Nazareth ever set out to do, by bringing together the many varied ideas of his times, which were sometimes conflicting, and forged them together into a viable whole. Into this religious stew he included "the Jewish, Greek, and Roman ideas of certain religious laws and duties that must be fulfilled with the Platonic idea and the ideas of Gnosticism and of the mystery religions of a mystical experience that lifts one up to and identifies one with God."[32] Paul has been called the second father of Christianity, and he was determined to make it a religion not just for Jews, but also for the whole world.

In Paul's earlier career as a Pharisee, he gleefully punished and executed Christians. He was responsible for the death of Stephen, among other disciples. Paul was a dogmatist, and any heresy of Jewish scripture was to be met with swift justice. It might be noted that he simply "hopped the fence," so to speak. One of the main reasons he extended

---

[30] Ibid.

[31] In some ways it did, if you consider that the religion of Paul is actually an entirely different theology than that which held by the original disciples.

[32] Artz, *Mind of the Middle Ages*, 58-59.

Christianity to the Gentiles was that he was almost universally hated in Jerusalem, from the Christians for his homicidal programs, and from the Jews as a traitor. He tried to preach in Jerusalem, once. A great mob formed and beat him nearly to death, and would have killed him had he not been saved by Roman soldiers. Many would have seen it to be just, considering what he had done to others.

In contradiction to Jesus, he declared the old Jewish laws to be unnecessary and offered salvation to Gentiles, which put him into further conflict with the Jewish Christians in Israel. Paul and Peter did not get along too well, and their theologies were quite opposed. Paul was something of a renegade in his teachings, and other disciples scoffed at his claim to be the first of disciples. In some ways his words were true, however, as he did more to establish Christianity and furthered the bounds of the sect more than any other, including Jesus himself.

Paul was a man of his own mind. He wrote the majority of the New Testament, and in all of it he quotes Jesus only once, and never refers to Jesus' sermons or teachings. It must be remembered that Paul started writing and teaching on Christianity *before* any of the four gospels of the New Testament were even written. The mystical Jew was no more as Paul had found his vehicle from which to attach his many varied ideas.

The Gospel of John

Some writers after Paul went even further from Judaism. The fourth gospel, the Gospel of John was written to appeal to Greek intellectuals and contains nothing of its Jewish roots. Written sometime after 100 A.D., it lays a great deal of emphasis upon gnosis (wisdom) and Logos, which is the word of the universe. The book of John begins: "In the beginning was the Word [Logos] and the Word was with God, and the Word was God."[33] Thus Jesus had now ceased to be a man at all, but the life force of the universe that the

---

[33] Holy Bible, John 1:1.

Greeks had been discussing for some time already. It does not contain the Sermon on the Mount or any reference to the parables of Jesus. It ceases to be a simple narrative and the entire setting is a grand cosmic drama written in philosophical terms, with everything in terms of "Light and Life and Darkness," which "was written not to supplement the first three gospels but to supplant them."[34]

What John is concerned with is not Jesus the man, but Jesus as an avatar, "exactly like an Indian or a Gnostic." The whole reason for the writing of the Gospel of John is to prove that Jesus is that avatar. John the Baptist is not introduced as a religious reformer, but as nothing more than the herald of the Christ.[35] "There was a man sent from God, whose name was John. The same came for a witness, to bear witness of the Light, that all men through him might believe. He was not that Light, but was sent to bear witness of that Light."[36]

One of the keys to the understanding the nature of the author is in John 1:41. "He first findeth his own brother Simon, and saith unto him, We have found the Messias, which is, being interpreted, the Christ."[37] Crowley understood the remarkableness of this verse, which is subtle. If in that time two Jews were speaking to each other, and one told the other that the Messiah had been found, there would have been no confusion at all, there would be no need for an interpretation or allusion. The author of John speaks of 'the Jews' as someone who is not a member, as someone who looks at Jews as foreigners. So John explains to his readers that Messiah means Christ, which Crowley says "is rather like explaining that the Prince of Wales is Balder the Beautiful."[38] The idea of a Christ and that of a Messiah are two wholly different things, a fact that has been all but lost on modern minds. The confusion mostly has arisen by the

---

[34] Artz, *Mind of the Middle Ages, 59.*
[35] Crowley, *Gospel*, 63.
[36] Holy Bible, John 1:6-8
[37] Ibid 1:41
[38] Crowley, *Gospel*, 62.

fact that etymologically both words mean 'anointed'. The idea of the Christ comes from Chaldea, India, China, and the Gnostics. It is not merely a person but a spiritual attainment, similar to that of a Buddha. The concept is actually at odds with the whole of Jewish theology.[39]

In contrast, a Messiah was very familiar to the Jews. Moses, Samson, and countless others had been Messiahs. A Messiah was basically a savior, just as Moses saved the Hebrews from the Egyptians and David saved them from the Palestinians. The common Jew wanted a messiah at that time, not to speak about religion, but to overthrow the Roman government. His lack of doing that made the Jews lose faith in him as a messiah; to them he did nothing useful at all. Campbell makes this point clear: "In earlier Jewish writings of the Day of the Messiah, the underlying notion had been simply of the restoration of the Jewish state under a king of the line of David, and the willing recognition, then, by all nations, of the truly Chosen People of God."[40]

The Jews envisioned this Messiah as a great man and hero, who would be supreme in his moral decisions as well. He would represent "the ultimate limit of man." He would be greater than the ordinary people, raised high above them, but the people would see his greatness and be willing to be his subjects. In the hierarchy, the Jews would say he is a little lower than God. If he were to rise up just slightly more then he would be God.[41] But this idea of rising up further was unthinkable to Jewish theology, which was and still is very monotheistic. Even though this step was but slight, from this Messiah and God, it was a step that could never be taken. The reason is that this man had already reached "the ultimate limit of man."

More importantly, in the distinction between a Messiah and a Christ, a Christ was something to be obtained and was a spiritual state. The Messiah was born into his

[39] Ibid., 65.
[40] Campbell, *Occidental Mythology*, 269.
[41] Ibid., 335.

46

path, and although very moral and spiritual, the physical plane was his arena of operation.

The book of John is a composite much more than the synoptic gospels, as it tries to layer Greek philosophy on top of a Jewish story. No other Jewish writing of the period even resembles it. The sophistication and intellectual background of the writer precludes the concept of 'a simple fisherman', and instead points to a very educated Greek or Phoenician.[42]

Syncretic Christianity

Christianity is an amazing thing, really. It is very unique. Not because there is someone dying for the world, which is really an old story. But the popularity of Christianity is directly linked to its universality. All throughout its history, any time it came into contact with another religion that competed with it, it brought in the beliefs and rituals of that religion until the local populace could not tell the difference.

The idea of a dying and resurrected god is one of the oldest stories in mythology. It had reverberated through the myths of various peoples for millennia. The one difference in the case of Jesus was that before him this myth was an ongoing, recurring cycle of life and death that was celebrated with rites and festivals at the appropriate times. But in Christian mythology, it was "an event in time, which had occurred but once, and marked the moment of the transfiguration of history." One such previous myth was of Dionysus, who is very closely linked to the Christ. Dionysus was born of a virgin in a cave, who was impregnated by a serpent. In his case, he was torn apart as an infant and then resurrected. In addition, Dionysus was the god of bread and wine, thus at his festivals these two were always consumed. Compare to this the communion of the church and the stories of Jesus begin to take on new light. Note too, that a dove impregnated the Virgin Mary. Both the dove and the

---

[42] Crowley, *Gospel*, 68.

serpent were symbols of the Mother Goddess in ancient times.[43]

The concept of the resurrection of the virtuous did not begin with Christianity either, but was originally conceived of by Zoraster. Zoraster's date is uncertain, but some sources surmise perhaps as early as 1500 B.C.E. Before him, people thought that they would go to a dull Hades, or some dim underworld. Zoraster developed the idea of his followers going to the skies and the unbelievers being put underground. Thus he also created the concept of hell, a place of punishment, rather than the underworld. He also predicted that there would be a future messiah figure that would vanquish evil and resurrect the dead.[44]

It should be obvious by now that to put any historical value on the New Testament is to act incredulous; to admire or study the ideas contained therein is not to admire the thoughts of the Hebrew mystic, and such an interpretation will lead one to misunderstanding and ignorance. A proper view is to understand the varied influences that came together, even at this early time, to form the religion, and thereby understand why Christianity represented everything during the Aeon of Osiris. The reason that this great synthesis took place at this time was due to the communication and travel afforded by the Roman Empire, which at no time previously in recorded history had been advanced to such levels. Thus were many cultures mixing and being compared, and it was natural for the various religions to find many similarities between their rites and legends, as all such myth is based on commonalities of the universal human experience. So, it was only prudent to join forces, to meld into a sort of trust rather than to waste resources in conflict. Those that synthesized survived, and those that did not, that insisted on religious purity became the fables of the past. Which is why a great coalition was formed, whether intentional or not, between "the priests of

---

[43] Campbell, *Occidental Mythology*, 27, 334.
[44] Bloom, *Omens of Millennium*, 7.

Mithras, Adonis, Attis, Osiris, Dionysus, Isis, Astarte, Venus, and many scores of others."[45]

Alexander the Great began this process of synthesis with the Hellenization of the East. Of the many lands he conquered, he showed not only a respect for their local deities, but earnestly desired to discover analogies between them. In this regard the Hellenists could be considered some of the first scholars of comparative religion. So it happened that the various deities began to be worshiped as equivalents of each other, such as Demeter and Isis, Thoth and Hermes, or Amoun and Zeus. Now there are numerous examples of cultures combining gods within their pantheon, especially in Egypt. But at no time in history before Alexander was there a systematic process of "transcultural syncretism." This is an example of the noble mind of the Greeks, who respected the individual, even if he were not Greek. In addition, the Greeks desired "an empire not of tyranny but of free men to the sphere of thought." The other great benefit of Alexander's campaign was that it brought the influence of India to the west, which is a most likely precursor for the numerous "gnostic, theosophical, and hermetic cults" which later emerged.[46]

The synthesis can be seen very clearly from the calendar of saints, where all the gods and goddesses that were encountered and considered important to pagans were incorporated in some form, and received the same honors and rituals as they always had, albeit under the form of angels, virgins, martyrs, or saints. In many cases these angels and virgins had the same name as the old deity, but in all cases had the same attributions. "Thus on the altar the Solar-phallic Crucifix is surrounded by six lights for the planets...Christmas is at the winter solstice, the birth of Christ put for the birth of the Sun."[47]

---

[45] Crowley, *Gospel*, 12-13.
[46] Campbell, *Occidental Mythology*, 240-41.
[47] Crowley, *Gospel*, 13.

Musings of a Thelemite

The Mythical Defamation of Pan

As has been seen, wherever Christianity encountered popular deities, they would often be incorporated into the Christian mythology by making him/her a saint, martyr, et cetera. There were two cases were this practice was avoided. The first case was with the serpent, which was examined above. The other case is Pan. Why was he not incorporated somehow into the pantheon of saints, and instead made symbolic of the Great Enemy Satan? This is an issue that needs to be explored fully here, not only to understand how Christian psychology has become twisted and unhealthy, but also to begin illustrating the differences between this old way and the new way of Horus.

The most obvious reason Pan was assaulted so vehemently was that in many ways he is an antithesis of what the Orthodox Church represented, and so with no amount of alteration could be reconciled to Christianity. It must be noted that it was later, after the priesthood had been established within Christianity, thus forming an ecclesiastical hierarchy as opposed to a spiritual movement, that the worship of Pan became a threat to the established Church.

    The proper way in which to understand Pan today is through the Tarot card "The Devil," which for the longest time was misunderstood as an evil force opposed to all forms of spirituality whatsoever, but which was finally redeemed by Aleister Crowley in his Thoth Tarot. As Crowley explains in *The Book of Thoth*, Pan is attributed to Capricorn and represents "creative energy in its most material form."[48] That sentence itself, although harmless, would be enough to cause most Christians to recoil in terror. First off, the idea of anything redeeming taking material form is contradictory to basic Christian theology, which views this world as a thing fallen from god and entirely

---

[48] Crowley, *Book of Thoth*, 105.

impure. Ultimately Pan is also connected to the energy and spirituality of sex, a concept that is both rejected and alien to Christendom. I cannot imagine a pious churchgoer identifying with "the goat leaping with lust upon the summits of earth."[49] Thus rejecting and having a serious complex with sex, the Christian can never understand the mystery of Pan. What is unknown is feared, then despised, then eventually termed as evil.

Indeed, even those of the west who do not consider themselves to be Christian often have a distorted view of sex. To understand a proper position we must go to the east, to the Tantric master Osho:

> Sex is there, the basic energy- the basic energy you are born through, born with. The basic cells of your being and of your body are sexual, so the human mind revolves around sex [...if you] fight you create a different center in yourself. The more you fight, the more you become integrated in a different center[...] Do not fight with it, transform it. Do not think in terms of enmity, be friendly to it. It is your energy. It is not evil, it is not bad. Every energy is just natural[...] You can make a block of it, a barrier, or you can make it a step[...] The ordinary mind is being destroyed by its own desires[...] Tantra says be aware of the desire, do not create any fight. Move into desire with full consciousness, and when you move into desire with full consciousness you transcend it.[50]

This western deviant psychology with sex is so deeply rooted that most people do not even realize it even when it is pointed out. Some could point to the blatant sexuality in movies, music, et cetera, but even in such cases those very people who enjoy it feel a bit of guilt, feel that they have "sinned." Westerners are often shocked upon finding that many of the temples in India have

---

[49] Ibid.
[50] Osho, *The Book of Secrets*, 17-18.

"pornographic scenes" displayed inside of their temples. The Christian says, "How can this be a temple with this filth here? This is a place of the devil!" The idea of sex being "dirty" is an alien concept to the eastern mind, or at least it was until the influence of the west, along with its psychoses.

Now we begin to see why the church felt the need to shut down the worship of Pan. Freud thought that all deviant psychology was a result of the repression of sexual urges. Although it might not be to quite that extent, he was definitely on to something. Of course, he lived during a time that table legs had to be covered, lest a man become aroused by their similarity of the furniture to the female ambulatory apparatus.

Musings of a Thelemite

In *Magick Without Tears*, Crowley gives us a hint at the potency of this sex energy:

> As all true Art is spontaneous, is genius, is utterly beyond all conscious knowledge or control, so also is sex. Indeed, one might class it as deeper still than Art; for Art does at least endeavour to find an intelligible means of expression. That is much nearer to sanity than the blind lust of the sex-impulse.[51]

It is an energy and drive that defies logical thought and religious prohibition concerning it. As St. Paul came to realize, "The spirit is willing but the flesh is weak." However he should have said, "the flesh is stronger than my mind." For if the flesh were truly weak, then it would be easy to repress it. Of course he made the first mistake of presuming to place his own will against the much greater Will of Pan. Pan isn't to be considered sane, and if you resist him, you will become completely deranged. Is it any surprise to anyone that those who molest children often did not have a healthy sex life? They have placed their will against Pan, and thus divorcing themselves from the All-Begetter, Pandemonium ensues. Crowley concludes that "attempts to suppress it are fatal," which seems obvious enough; what perhaps is more difficult for the student is to avoid the opposite mistake of placing sex on too high of level, which Crowley says is "false and futile."[52] This seems to be epidemic in the west today, where many people are obsessed with sex and sex is used to sell everything. This type of obsession is just as dangerous as suppression, but with differing effects. It blinds those obsessed from deeper aspects of others and reduces everything to materialism and flesh. The flesh can indeed be a part of the spiritual life, contrary to Christian belief, but like everything else it must be balanced. To obsess with the flesh above all else creates a person who is both callous and shallow.

---

[51] Crowley, *Magick Without Tears*, 130.
[52] Ibid.

The Three Aeons

It must be understood that sex is an amoral force. It can empower the student or hang him. Remember that Osho teaches "Do not fight with it, transform it." Notice that this is an energy that must be transformed. Energy in itself is nothing if it is not used to some purpose. The only truly correct use for energy is fulfilling the Great Work, which to the vulgar means enlightenment, and for the Adept Abrahadabra. Osho says to "move into desire with full consciousness," which would be in total agreement with Crowley who warns against either suppressing it or elating it. The path of the student should be down the middle pillar, balance. Sex is a ship that cannot be rightly steered, but one can know where one is sailing. To try and pull it one way or another is the danger.

Primary Attributes of Christianity

The Death Cult

The concept of death became paramount to those religions belonging to the Aeon of Osiris, and thus most religions today are wholly concerned with death. This is most true of Christianity, which is the apex of the Aeon of Osiris and the chief death cult. As was written by St. Paul:

> Know ye not, that so many of us as were baptized into Jesus Christ were baptized into his death? Therefore we are buried with him by baptism into death: that like as Christ was raised up from the dead by the glory of the Father, even so we also should walk in the newness of life. For if we have been planted together in the likeness of his death, we shall be also in the likeness of his resurrection: Knowing this, that our old man is crucified with him, that the body of sin might be destroyed, that henceforth we should not serve sin. For he that is dead is freed from sin[53].

---

[53] Holy Bible, Rom 6:3-8

I imagine few Christians can appreciate the humor of that last sentence. Anyway, you can turn to almost any section of the New Testament, especially the epistles of Paul, and will find the word death, dead, and die repeated over and over. The Christians gloried in death, and although modern believers might be a little more protective of their life, those of the first century were anxious to be "killed all day long; we are accounted as sheep for the slaughter"[54] and were "always delivered unto death for Jesus' sake..."[55] always believing that "...to die is gain."[56]

Christianity teaches it glory to die to Jesus' sake, that this life is filth compared to the life hereafter. All pleasures of the flesh are shunned. Paul wrote that all the troubles of the world are not worth one moment of heavenly bliss. The crucifix, a symbol of execution and death as much as the noose, has become the symbol of the religion. The baptism, with the symbolic death and rebirth are very similar to the Dionysian rites. A saved Christian is "reborn." Jesus himself is associated with the sun. Thus Jesus replaced the father-sky god and incorporated the additional ideas of the sun and death, just as Osiris did.

The Slave Religion

There is a great attraction to Christianity, and this attraction has made it the most widespread religion the world has ever known. Many of the Christians see the time when "the word" shall be proclaimed to the ends of the earth drawing near. One of the pleasures of Christianity is that it allows the follower to be weak. I know this from personal experience. Even though I put a great deal of restriction on myself, the root of it all was an underdeveloped Will. The Christian attack is two-fold. First it causes you to feel as though you were a vile sinner and a general piece of shit. This is the sin complex. Then when you feel like a dog wouldn't bother to piss on you, you find out

[54] Ibid., Rom 8:36
[55] Ibid., 2 Cor 4:10-11
[56] Ibid, Phil 1:21

that a god himself came down and was executed for your sins. You can cast all your cares upon him. The first shall be last and the last shall be first. So since by this time you are pretty sure you are last, this is a pretty good bonus. Yea, the bigger the fool the bigger the throne in heaven. So it really appeals to the mob, for the worse of a person you are, then the greater the glory; the greater the sin, then greater is the forgiveness. It feeds on the ego in a demented sort of way so that you take pride in being base. Christians compete with each other proclaiming how sinful and worthless they all are, and get really upset if someone manages to show that they are more sinful and worthless than themselves. To this day, the entire religion continues to astound me.

Is Christianity True?

I have often been asked, 'was/is the formula of Christianity true? And if so, how can it now be untrue?' The question is not of truth, but of usefulness. What is useful becomes true, at least for all practical purposes. We are accustomed, in the west, of thinking of truth with a capital "T". But many things in life are not so clear cut and defined, the least of all science, which makes the pretension of exactness and absolute verifiable truth. To understand this better it is necessary to look at the foundation of scientific theory itself. Science questions everything, and by its methods either proves or disproves things. But where is the science of science? Why do we not question the method itself? It seems to work, as all around us we have the products of science, we have cars and electricity, et cetera ad infinitum, and so we consider science to be "true". But that which works is not necessarily true in absolute. So we must go to the core of science, which begins with a hypothesis.

The formation of a hypothesis is a very mystifying event. Once it is in existence, then it can be tested and through testing it can be seen whether or not it holds truth. But before it is tested, it must come into being. Where do these hypotheses come from? A scientist will be sitting there and in a flash it hits him. It comes from nowhere, an unexplained source, unexplained by science at least. Einstein said regarding the laws of the cosmos that "there is no logical path to these laws; only intuition, resting on sympathetic understanding of experience can reach them..." No logical path? These words seem extraordinary coming from the greatest scientist of the twentieth century. What is even more odd is that the method he proposes is of "intuition" and "sympathetic understanding," which would, on the surface, seem to be diametrically opposed to the method of science. Indeed, if the quote were not attributed, would one not rather think that it were the method of poetry? Robert Pirsig mentions how Phaedrus's original issues with science came from trying to understand the nature of hypotheses. Phaedrus noticed that as he was testing a hypothesis a number of other hypotheses would come to mind, and as he was testing these even more would come to him. This increase was so rapid that they piled up much quicker than could be tested. He found this amusing at first and coined a law stating, "The number of rational hypotheses that can explain any given phenomenon is infinite."[57]

He found his law rather humorous and enjoyed the fact that he would never run out of hypotheses, but it was a few months later that Phaedrus "began to have some doubts about the humor or benefits of it." It had not dawned on him earlier the significance of what he had discovered. After soberly considering this matter in a new light he concluded: "if true, that law is not a minor flaw in scientific reasoning. The law is completely nihilistic. It is a catastrophic logical disproof of the general validity of all scientific method!"[58] The reason for his dramatic realization is that the business of science in theory is to discover the workings of things, to form theories and to test them, thereby discovering the truths of the universe. But if the rate of hypotheses grows faster than they can be tested, then it becomes obvious that

---

[57] Pirsig, *Zen*, 99.
[58] Ibid.

all hypotheses cannot ever be tested. Without being tested "the results of any experiment are inconclusive and the entire scientific method falls short of its goal of establishing proven knowledge."[59]

Einstein is not much help to the cause of science here either. He merely states that "at any given moment" one of the hypotheses will prove "superior to the rest." Notice, not true, merely superior, and even this superiority is limited to "any given moment." Thus what we like to think of as "Truth" is subject to time. What is true can change, even with science. Truth is not permanent, inviolate, nor sacred. Phaedrus continued looking into the subject of scientific truths and what he found amazed him. He discovered that the length of time something remained a "truth" was inverse to the amount of study that was being done. Scientific research, rather than causing truth and knowledge to be more stable, in fact cause it to become much more volatile. In older times truth hardly ever changed and thus had a semblance of permanency. How long was it a truth that the earth was flat and that the sun revolved around it? But now, theories are constantly being replaced. At one time a law of science would last centuries, but now it is lucky to survive five years. As hypotheses are introduced with greater intensity, they quickly replace others that came before. It is not that one is true and the other false, but rather that one is more useful. As Pirsig remarks, "the more you look, the more you see."[60]

The issue of truth is also illuminated by Pirsig's look at the history of geometry. In the beginning we have Euclidian geometry. This system had been used for some time, although one aspect of it gave mathematicians a great deal of trouble. This aspect was Euclid's fifth postulate, which no one was able to demonstrate. The postulate states, "through a given point there is not more than one parallel line to a given straight line." So one had an aspect of

---

[59] Ibid., 100.
[60] Ibid., 100-01.

mathematics that couldn't be demonstrated, but at the same time couldn't be thrown out, because to do so would mean eliminating a huge portion of mathematics.

It must be pointed out that even though this postulate could not be demonstrated, the entire system of geometry worked and was used by architects and engineers. It was in the first part of the nineteenth century that two men, Bolyai and Lobachevski reversed Euclid's fifth postulate.

"Lobachevski assumes at the start that through a given point can be drawn two parallels to a given straight." Everything else he left the same. He worked out a whole system of geometry from these facts, and it fit together and worked flawlessly. In trying to demonstrate that "the fifth postulate is irreducible to simpler axioms," Lobachevski at first didn't realize what he had just done. It soon dawned on him, and on the rest of the scientific world, that there were two systems of perfect geometry that contradicted each other at their very root.

"Mathematics, the cornerstone of scientific certainty, was suddenly uncertain."[61] Things did not stop there. Sometime later a German named Riemann formed another system of geometry that contradicted the previous two. As to the question of which system is true, Jules Henri Poincare stated, "the question has no meaning." It would be similar to declaring the Cartesian coordinates more true than the polar coordinates, or asking whether the metric system or the avoirdupois system were true. "One geometry can not be more true than another; it can only be more convenient. Geometry is not true, it is advantageous."[62]

Therefore, the question is not whether the Aeon of Osiris was true in any absolute sense. The proper answer might be that it was the best option at the time for

---

[61] Ibid., 233-37.

[62] Ibid. The above also can be applied to such diverse questions as seem to plague the beginner, such as "Do the gods really exist or are they only an aspect of higher consciousness?" "Is Buddhism true?" "Is this an autonomous force?" And my favorite, "Where did you get that information?" *Et cetera ad infinitum et nausea.*

understanding that which was divine. It was better than the formula of Isis, and the formula of the Aeon of Horus is better than Osiris. What is also explicit in these statements is that this is not a final destination, where we are now. If the human consciousness is to advance, then eventually we must move past Horus as well. But that is far enough in the future that it doesn't need much attention at the moment. Indeed, it is only now that the energies of the Aeon of Horus are coming to fruition. He is still the crowned and conquering child.

Returning to the question of the truth of Osiris and Christianity, it should be clear now that to understand the past age is pertinent, but that the methods no longer need be used. It would be similar to yoking up a couple of oxen to a wagon in the morning to go to work. At one time, it was a pretty good way of doing things, much preferable to walking and carrying loads. Was riding in a wagon the true way of doing things? Is there a proper way to travel? It seems facetious to ask such questions, only because we have no sacredness of traveling. To other cultures of other times it would have been a very serious question. Proper understanding will come from seeing the foolishness of ascribing sacredness to any truths as well.

The proper way for one to approach the older Christian writings is as one might to mythology. There are parables and lesson that can be learned from it, but it should also be kept at arms length. It certainly should not be considered history in any sense of the term. It also must be understood that Christianity as it stands today is an infectious disease. The Bible has been formed and fitted for the masses and the vast majority of the mysteries have been covered up. Crowley remarks that the versions of Christ of the many churches today are merely "the machine-gods of all fraud and oppression, being stolen and prostituted from that Christ in whom our fathers in the Gnosis strove to synthesize the warring Gods of Syria, Greece, Chaldea,

Rome, and Egypt."[63] Since that time Christianity has lost practically all of its hold on truth, a mere social-club given out to appease the conscious of the simple minded, having lost all of its deeper meaning, the outer church holds mere symbols without knowledge of what those symbols mean. As Nietzsche wrote, "Books for all the world are always foul-smelling books: the smell of small people clings to them. Where the people eat and drink, even where they venerate, it usually stinks. One should not go to church if one wants to breathe pure air."[64]

The paradigm of Christianity can be difficult to escape for many. It still has a strong pull due to the length of time that it has pervaded our consciousness. Anything that has been quoted and referred to for such a long time gains the appearance of truth, despite the ridiculousness of the book, the contradictions, the immorality. It is very interesting to view an eastern man's opinion of the Bible or of Christianity who has not grown up with it intravenously being injected into his consciousness. Often he is repulsed by the vulgarity and filthiness of the book that so many westerners consider to be "the Word of God."

Horus states: "With my Hawk's head I peck out the eyes of Jesus as he hangs upon the cross."[65] It must be understood that this is because his viewpoint is no longer valid. Crowley explains this is because of "his Magical Gesture of self-sacrifice."[66] This idea is represented by the Tarot card XII: The Hanged Man, which in the Aeon of Osiris "represented the supreme formula of adeptship."[67] This supreme idea was of self-sacrifice, to take up one's cross daily. Through self-deprivation of the self, one could fully submit to the divine. But as Crowley put it, "this idea of sacrifice is, in the final analysis, a wrong idea."[68] Wrong

---

[63] Crowley, *Gospel*, 16.
[64] Nietzsche, *Beyond Good & Evil*, 43.
[65] Crowley, *Book of the Law*, III:51.
[66] Crowley, *The Law is for All*, 169.
[67] Crowley, *Book of Thoth*, 96-97.
[68] Ibid.

because it is no longer necessary or useful. Nuit declares: "I give unimaginable joys on earth: certainty, not faith, while in life, upon death; peace unutterable, rest, ecstasy; nor do I demand aught in sacrifice."[69] Crowley goes on to say that "it should be the chiefest aim of the wise to rid mankind of the insolence of self-sacrifice, of the calamity of chastity; faith must be slain by certainty, and chastity by ecstasy."[70]

Despite the quaintness with which I look back on Christianity, the truth is that we are not yet out of its influence. The snake of Christianity still hangs on by one rotten fang, and lashes its body about, still trying to grip the life of the body of Ra-Hoor-Khuit. Christianity, once a proper path to the divine has now become cancerous, and displays all of the most nauseous qualities man is capable of. Now it has caused, and is still causing an "eclipse of the spirit," which Nietzsche described as a "characteristic of noble cultures." In exchange, those who are infected by this eclipse let "much suffering be seen and heard that one formerly bore and hid," the masses are prone to a "moral hypocrisy," a black stench to all of noble souls. This weak man of today tries to distinguish himself "not by means of morality, but by means of the herd virtues: pity, consideration, moderation" which leads to a weakening of the Will.[71]

The Aeon of Horus

With the coming of the Aeon of Osiris, the idea of the Great Mother was superseded by the formula of IAO, which represents the dying god, and "made the male, dying to himself in the act of love, the engineer of the continued life of the race." Matriarchy was no more, and there was no higher deed than self-sacrifice. But just as night is no longer seen to be the death of the sun, so "death does not end life; it is a temporary phase of life as night and winter are of terrestrial activity."[72]

---

[69] Crowley, *Book of the Law*, I:58.
[70] Crowley, *Book of Thoth*, 96-97.
[71] Nietzsche, *Will to Power*, 41.
[72] Crowley, *Confessions*, 795-96.

Musings of a Thelemite

The three Aeons can be represented by the three Hebrew mother letters. Isis is symbolized by Mem, water and the feminine female. Osiris is seen in Aleph, air and the feminine male. The Aeon of Horus is represented by Shin, which is both fire and spirit and the masculine male. Thus our Aeon is one of energy and action, both of the sword and the spirit. It is a time of liberation of thought and a freedom for the soul. The history of the Aeon of Horus is as of yet short, for we are writing our history now, with our deeds in the world. The most pronounced incident that has occurred was the writing of *The Book of the Law*, which I will detail in full in my essay 'Thelema'.

All paths lead to Horus. No matter how much a man may try to escape it, he must realize it is impossible. Aleister Crowley did not create *The Book of the Law* or Thelema. The Aeon of Horus is bigger than Crowley, and even bigger than Thelema. It is not a spiritual movement, it is an Aeon. It can and probably will be demonstrated in other holy books besides Liber CCXX. There is no need for a unified theory of the Aeon among all participants. In the Aeon of Osiris, there was both Christianity and Buddhism, which although relying on the same formula, were starkly different in many regards.

In the Aeon of Horus the male spark gains mastery over itself so that it may deny the mother, and thus deny the will to death. Also is the disregard of the hive state and a true ability of independence. This evolution also explains the relation of the sexes throughout history. During the Aeon of Isis, the great mother held total power. There was the beginning of the male spark, but it was too weak to be independent. Thus we have Harpocrates in mythology. This type of state can still be observed in hive animals such as bees. The female dominates everything from the top down, and the male has no use beyond his ability to generate sperm. After reproduction, the male dies.

During the Aeon of Osiris, when the male broke free of the hive, he retaliated with all of his force. The hive state was thrown down, and males competed between themselves for dominance. The females were thrown into complete submission and used for breeding purposes, much as the males had been before. The chief difference was that the male independence allowed for wars and conflict, thus allowing development. The hive had succeeded to such an extent that it was locked in time. Necessity is the mother of invention. During this time, there was a great distrust and hatred of woman that contrasted with the urge to put woman on a pedestal as perfection. The urge to rape conflicted with the urge to forever preserve the virgin. These conflicting urges stemmed from man's newly won independence, his ignorance of what to do with it, and his confusion as to what to do with the woman, who was still the emissary of the great mother. This development can also be seen when a man gains independence from his physical mother. But in all of this, man was still serving the great mother. Even though he had broken free to some extent, the wars between men, the competition, this served the mother's purpose of survival of the fittest. Also, even though the human woman was devoid of all power (in male terms), she still held immense control through more subtle means. Thus we have the face that sailed a thousand ships.

Man continued to struggle with woman, not knowing what to do with her. But now god was a man, even though the virgin mother was slipped in. Even during this time, woman was man's redemption. A good example of this was seen in *Paradise Lost*, where even though Eve causes man's downfall, it is through her seed that man will be redeemed. In the New Testament, Mary is depicted as the vehicle for man's redemption.

Musings of a Thelemite

Mary as Mother of God

Then came the end of the world and the Aeon of Horus. Here, the male spark gains solar consciousness. If this fire, (which is the element of the Aeon) can burn hot enough, it can become independent of the great mother. No longer will man throw himself to sacrifice to the great mother, he has learned the futility of it. Also, the relationship between the man and the great mother, and consequently the woman, is now realized. Woman is the portal. Man, by necessity must purge himself of the great mother's influence, and become the crowned and conquering child. Man must not oppress and stultify woman. She is his help-mate, and if her will becomes his, as the moon reflects the sun, then she will no longer be the servant of the great mother. Upon breaking her servitude to the mother, she becomes man's ally and true partner in this new Aeon. And then mankind has become emancipated and can do its Will.

The Aeon of Horus has seen two world wars, which is fitting, as he is a god of war. It has seen the splitting of the atom, and nuclear destruction. In literature everything has pushed toward pessimistic postmodernism and existentialism. In general, our technology and power is moving forward but the soul of humanity is falling apart. In older times, the masses at least nominally believed in Christianity. Since that religion is now seen to be ridiculous to modern man, he has no spirit. He believes in nothing. Life is a bitter experience to grab and live and die. During Victorian times this materialistic attitude led to the creation of Marxism. Marx made a number of wise observations, but failed in providing an answer to these problems. Weaklings today still advocate the doctrines of Marx. Now we stand in the twenty first century, where terrorist blow things up, and we talk peace with them. Then the terrorist laughs and blows up the diplomats. As Emerson noted, "Power is, in nature, the measure of right."[73]

The great spirits in the Aeon of Horus are born in bondage. They are cast into nihilism by the herd. Chains of feminism, political correctness, racial cheerleaders, peaceniks, all those belonging to the school of resentment seek to stultify humanity by a process of leveling that crushes those who have the soul of an aristocrat. Not until these weaklings are slain philosophically, or in actuality, can the kings be free. Democracy, which originated as a way of freedom, has become a method of bondage by the weak. The feminists to the lions! A thousand times I say. Damn them and their crapulent creeds. Every man and woman is a star, which is true enough, but does this change the nature of a man? Every man and woman is a star, but remember that a black hole is a star as well.

Friedrich Nietzsche, Prophet and Saint of Thelema

Friedrich Nietzsche, that great saint and prophet of Thelema, despised these weaklings; he very aptly termed them as the "levelers- these falsely so-called 'free spirits' – being eloquent and prolifically scribbling slaves of the democratic taste and its 'modern ideas'; they are all human beings without solitude."[74] Crowley himself admitted that

---

[73] Emerson, *The Portable Emerson*, 153.
[74] Nietzsche, *Beyond Good & Evil*, 54.

he did not live up to the ideas of the Aeon sufficiently. For that we cannot offer any blame. He did far more than the average man. But to hear a voice of Thelema ring so true as to cause one to shutter, one need only turn to Nietzsche. Despite what modern interpreters may say, Thelema is an elitist philosophy. The Law is for all, as we say, because as Thelemites we truly wish for every man to realize his true potential, and live as the true director of his fate. But in reality, how many are brave enough to do this?

Friedrich Nietzsche

Nietzsche saw with the eyes of a prophet what was coming. He saw the Aeon of Horus that would come, and that those of Osiris would have to be destroyed. There are many who parade about today and speak of freedom or liberty, when in fact they wish no such thing, wanting only to enslave the masses with the formulas of the old Aeon. Do not be fooled by such deceptions. "What they would like to strive for with all their powers is the universal green-pasture happiness of the herd, with security, lack of danger, comfort, and an easier life for everyone; the two songs and doctrines which they repeat most often are 'equality of rights' and 'sympathy for all that suffers' – and suffering itself they take for something that must be abolished."[75]

How often have these songs been repeated by those disciples of resentment today: the feminists, Marxists, racial cheerleaders, and all the crapulence of political correctness. Perhaps you find yourself agreeing with them. Perhaps you are not a Thelemite, and would do better in a liberal minded humanitarian church. Horus has declared, "Now let it be first understood that I am a god of War and of Vengeance. I shall deal hardly with them;"[76] "Mercy let be off: damn them who pity! Kill and torture; spare not; be upon them!"[77] Finally he states, "Despise also all cowards; professional soldiers who dare not fight, but play; all fools despise!"[78]

I need neither permission nor affirmation from fools. Horus speaks for me. For those who would question my right to speak thus, remember the words of Nuit, "The word of Sin is Restriction [...] thou hast no right but to do thy will. Do that, and no other shall say nay. For pure will, unassuaged of purpose, delivered from the lust of result, is every way perfect."[79] By this do not mistake that I somehow place myself over other true seekers and Thelemites, which would be ridiculous. If you be one of us, I cannot harm you. So let us fight as brothers.

---

[75] Ibid.

[76] Crowley, *Book of the Law*, III:3

[77] Ibid., III:18.

[78] Ibid., III:57-58.

[79] Ibid., I:41-43

Thelema

The core of Thelema is *The Book of the Law*, which was written down in 1904 by Aleister Crowley. The events leading up to its writing are an interesting affair, and although I risk presenting superfluous information, I think it pertinent to briefly present how the book came into being.

Crowley relates the detailed circumstances in his autobiography, *Confessions*. It began in 1904 while Crowley and his wife Rose were on their honeymoon in Cairo, Egypt. Crowley had been trying to summon sylphs for his wife to see. Apparently things didn't work out right because she couldn't see them, but instead started chanting, "They are waiting for you." These two facts together annoyed Crowley. The next day, while repeating the operation, his wife started up again, this time adding, "It is all about the child." She told him that he had offended Horus. This somewhat caught Crowley's attention, because he had always disliked Horus, seeing him as a force of unintelligent violence. He also had a grudge against him because Mathers had always been highly devoted to Mars. But these were facts that his wife was unlikely to know, as she had not had any magickal training at all, and in fact thought the whole business was balderdash.[80]

Although being the one who wrote down the words, Crowley was not truly the author. He wrote the words that were spoken to him by the messenger Aiwaz. Aleister Crowley was the witness to the end of the old Aeon of Osiris. He recorded the words that were spoken to him each day from noon and one p.m. on April 8th, 9th, and 10th in the year 1904. It was during that time that the principles of the new Aeon were pronounced to him. The Aeon is to remain in place for 2,000 years. Thus did the new times begin.

The angel Aiwaz was the messenger who told Crowley the words of the gods. There are three chapters of

---

[80] Crowley, *Confessions*, 393-94.

the sacred text, which are a communication from Nuit, Hadit, and Ra-Hoor-Khuit in that order. Seen in a metaphysical sense, Nuit is space, Hadit is movement, and Ra-Hoor-Khuit is the interplay between these forces.

Thelema could be considered a religion, a philosophy, a method of enlightenment like Kabbala, or a combination of all of them. It can also be seen as a law of physics, as an observation of the way things are. The core of Thelema is the acknowledgement of the new Aeon, and the principles by which it is governed. The chief book of Thelema is called *The Book of the Law*, which is a rather short work of three chapters, written down in 1904 by Aleister Crowley.

The Three Deities of Thelema
The first chapter is dictated by Nuit, the starry goddess of the skies. It is she who I will return to when I shuffle off this mortal coil. I may remain with her, or I may exit her womb and return. She is my lover and the mother of all. She states "I am the blue-lidded daughter of Sunset; I am the naked brilliance of the voluptuous night-sky. To me! To me!"[81] She represents everything that is best in woman. She has some allusions to Mary, mother of Jesus. But she is not chaste. In her sexual nature she could be likened to Aphrodite. Nuit is very sexually aggressive, but all in love. She says "Love is the law, Love under will." The desire to unite with her should be the same as the desire to unite with a lover. Crowley warned to not let this desire get out of control, however. Nuit is also much like a feminine Dionysus. She tells us to drink and take love where we may, but always to her. Nuit is the higher place that we may ascend to. She is the sky, the heavens, and therefore a symbol of enlightenment.

The second chapter is the voice of Hadit. Hadit is the lover of Nuit and at the center of all and everyone. He is the point and Nuit is the circle. He is the physical aspect of us,

---

[81] All quotes from the gods taken from *The Book of the Law*.

which longs to break free and join Nuit, which is that above. Hadit is secret and can never be truly known. He can be likened to Thoth in some ways, as he is the secret intelligence. Hadit states, "I am the flame that burns in every heart of man, and in the core of every star. I am life, and the giver of life, yet therefore is the knowledge of me the knowledge of death." He is the only one of the three who had no anthropomorphic form at all. He is simply the point, or the winged circle, or the solar serpent. An atom is a good visual for him, and another connection to science and knowledge. For without science, we would have no conception of an atom or even know that it exists. Hadit is directed thought. Even though he will never be truly known, so will knowledge of our universe never be complete. But that is no reason to not pursue truth and understanding.

Nuit being the infinitely large and Hadit being the infinitely small creates a great amount of tension. It is from this tension that the child is born, Ra-Hoor-Khuit. We are Ra-Hoor-Khuit. Anyone born after 1904 is in fact an incarnation of the god. He is the total of the human race and the archetype of humanity. We should all follow him, for in doing so we follow ourselves. He does not exist beyond us. It could be argued that all gods can be seen as such. I agree, but Ra-Hoor-Khuit is the most important god right now. He represents all of humanity, not just a small space of certain consciousness. So in this fashion, he is of the utmost importance. That is why he has many different forms. These are for the different stages of the individual man or woman. He is the crowned and conquering child of the Aeon, just as we are only children in these new times. As we grow, so shall he. As we learn, so shall he. He is symbolized as a hawk-headed god enthroned, and is the representative of the new Aeon. His message is very important to the human race:

> There is success. I am the Hawk-Headed Lord of Silence & of Strength; my nemyss shrouds the nigh-blue sky. Hail! ye twin warriors about the pillars of the world! for your time is nigh at hand. I am the Lord of the Double Wand of Power; the

Thelema

wand of the Force of Coph Nia-but my left hand
is empty, for I have crushed an Universe; &
nought remains.[82]

Knowing the True Will

Every person has a True Will, also known as the
HGA.[83] It is the core of our being. "Do what thou wilt" does
not mean simply do whatever you want. It means doing
your True Will. The True Will is the True Self. It is the voice
that whispers to you when no one else is there. The problem
is that we have all been taught many things in this life, and
are influenced by many people. So we have many thoughts
and voices circling around in our heads. But the True Will is
still there, and once a person hones in on it, and realizes it,
then he shall succeed at everything. The True Will is the Will
of the universe, so when we follow it we are following our
proper course in life.

Until we take responsibility for ourselves, to
understand and act out our True Will, we are bound to fail
in our pursuits in this life. We of Thelema must be strong
and free to know our True Will; only then can we proceed
correctly. Only those who fear shall fail. Therefore we must
be without fear, and to accomplish the Great Work that is
our birthright and our destiny. Ra-Hoor-Khuit has no
tolerance for cowards and weaklings, those afraid to offend
others and tip-toe through the world. I have no tolerance for
tolerance. The Christians to the lions! A thousand times I
say. We shall have no more of this nonsense.

When we are doing our True Will, there is nothing
that can hinder us from going forth on our holy course. All
of the elements are at our disposal. The universe bends knee
and offers its hand. We all have our own orbit to follow and
no man shall tell us otherwise. The chains of darkness and
deceit must be smitten away so that we may bask in the
glory that is. By following the True Will, one shall gain
freedom from the darkness and ignorance of the many false

---

[82] Crowley, *Book of the Law*, III: 69-72.
[83] Holy Guardian Angel

73

paths and false teachers that seek only our slavery. We shall walk unhindered.

An Account of the
Holy Guardian Angel

Throughout the countless eons, even as Jacob did wrestle with god, so have men wrestled with the true nature of Will and ego. Western Analytical philosophy uses its impotent faculties in an attempt to fabricate concrete answers. But this Tower of Babel that they have constructed will not reach god. Our modern Babylonians are guided by ego and do not have the gumption to behold the ascending ladder. They are not warriors, but professional soldiers and cowards who will fight only for pay. The true nature of Will can only be discerned by the diligent seeker who has the heart of the poet and the soul of a god.

And the modern science of the day has defiled the entire issue, sticking their caramel covered fingers into our doctrines while licking their greedy lips, thinking themselves worthy to toy with that which is greater than themselves, and placing our sacred totems under the profanity of their microscopes and instruments, these weak and scared men who have seen a hair of the universe and who propose to present us with a complete diagnosis on the body of god: cowards and blasphemers all, ready to fornicate themselves for the smallest scrap of praise. All ye who would take the name scientist and scoff at the mystic beware, for the universe scoffs in return.

The main distinctions which must be made when approaching the sacred topic of the Will is that there are two forms distinct; it is imperative to not confuse these separate forces, for from such improper fraternization comes the thousand devils of the flesh which will drag the would-be seeker into the pits of the lowest hell, and he will have to suffer along in the habitations of the yuppies, the bourgeois, the "happy" middle-class, and espouse effluvial Tartuffery for the remainder of his days. One must break the programming that has continually raped our native thoughts for the sole purpose of making us the

75

somnambulant minions of the demiurge. The location of this mundane propaganda is within the ego, that forward consciousness that is the primary apparatus by which we operate within and manipulate the reality in which we live in. But the profanity of the epicene scientists, with their continual rote sermons, is that they would have us believe that the ego is the highest form of mind and proceed to dissect it as if it were a seizure-ridden amphibian upon their steel plate. But even this butchering they consider to be complimentary, for to them it is all deterministic chemical reactions which we cannot control except through further chemical reactions in the form of small egg-like pellets that worship in the churches of Paxil and Ritalin.

I, as a visionary mystic of the highest order of self, urinate on both of these churches, refuse to seek answers within the forms that reside in the refuse of the material trash heap, instead choosing the ancient path of the medicine man, the shaman, who speaks directly with the divine; not restricted by church doctrine, not enslaved by forms and tradition, nay in fact pushing to destroy all tradition that seeks to limit or slow the divine message of purity.

This weak trash-fouled ego is not the source of self. We are indeed born pre-willed by the force that causes Terra firma to circumambulate sol, and this force I call either the True Will of the Holy Guardian Angel, to be most sharply distinguished from the false will of the ego. Many of the goals of this false will have been stacked upon our heads by the fools of this world, making us nothing more than the synthetic products of our environment. Most men are perfectly happy living their lives as groveling, drooling, lowly slaves who want nothing more than democracy, peace, happiness and security. They speak of equal rights and community, these epicene weaklings who do not have an ounce of probity per ten pounds of dumb flesh.

There is another type of man who is opposite of, and an enemy to the slave. He is the hero-king of myth, the elite few, Übermensch, Seth's children, those of the true inner church, Illuminati, Nephilim; these are the kings and rightful

An Account of the Holy Guardian Angel

sentinels of reality. It is for these numerically minuscule giants of the soul that I spend my many hours upon the paper: you the illuminated, my brothers.

The kings are capable of stripping away the numerous false influences of false satellites that alter the true orbit of the soul. The soul, the True Will, this guides one according to one's proper course in life. The True Will is the source of all imagination, beauty, art, spiritual experience- pure and distilled cosmic forces that a bleeding science strains to contain, but realizing it cannot, dismisses as "frivolous." Imagination is a hurricane to the small ships of knowledge, which shall be beaten upon the shore again and again until only splinters remain floating in the frothing surf of consciousness.

The eastern teachers will tell a person that he must destroy the ego so he may be one with god. I interpret this to mean, "Destroy the ego so that you may actualize the True Will." But destroy the ego? This is pure madness my friend, born of the ascetic delusions of desert deprivations. Never in a multitude of universes, if they were allowed to progress from the primal spark until the final yawn of cold death, not even then could you accomplish this feat. For what these Old Eastern chaps have failed to figure out while pressing their visages into the limestone, and which I have stumbled upon in a rampage of inebriation, is that the ego is the device of communication, the bridge if you will, in- between that which above and that which is below. The ego is the little will. The trouble is that he is an ungrateful bastard son who envies the deeds of Oedipus, and who has been gallivanting around deficient of the providence from the True Will, and thus is not the smaller homunculus that it was conceived to be. As above, so below. If it is not so, then the soul is in dissolution from existence and men lead an empty life of profanity- often right in the god-forsaken church. No, the ego cannot be destroyed, for to do so would leave the True Will no vehicle. Rather than destruction, drive toward assimilation. Simplicity, simplicity, simplicity! Let the dead bury the dead! Forge the soul and will into a

razor's edge; cut away the superfluous matter that is
unnecessary to True purpose and destiny.

Purpose- ah, there's the rub. Everyone has a
purpose from the president to the plumber. Often the
cylindrical engineer has greater purpose than he who holds
supreme executive power. The slaves do not concern
themselves with their purpose, being overly concerned with
bending knee to the whims of others and society who in turn
are the somnambulant sluts of the demiurge. The slaves are
daily vexed with what organic matter to stuff down their
digestive tubes, what pieces of petroleum-based material
from which to cover their vulgar forms, which of the other
slaves they will rendezvous with, or whether a famous slave
revealed her purulent mammary flesh flaps to the gaping
eye of the camera to deliver it to the coma-like petulant
masses with their gaping orifices. All of this crapulence is
distraction and irreverent irrelevance. Focus. That is the
byword of kings. To do otherwise is to voluntarily throw
one's self into the writhing filthy masses of omnivores.

The impediment to action advances action. What
stands in the way becomes the way. A king can also be
brought low, by mistakenly believing that situational
adversity can prevent one's actions. But the adversity is not
a wall but a rapidly flowing river that, although perhaps is
not the first-class travel of the bourgeois, then at least it is a
much more rapid method of obtaining the proper
correspondence.

Discord or concord? There is no difference. Our
purpose must follow whatever path is available until one
realizes that there is no path.

There are numerous ways of perceiving a causal of
purpose. One might be called that of Logos. By this I mean
the pull of fate obeys the whims of an impersonal cosmos in
a deterministic sort of way, that our lives are pre-ordained
for the greater good and balance of the universe. In the end
$1 + (-1) = 0$. The stoics adopted this approach with a dash of
freewill. If a dog is tied to a cart he can either run or be
dragged. He has the choice, but his path is inevitable. In

An Account of the Holy Guardian Angel

some ways this is similar to a spider in the mouth, but preferable to the abyss of Da'ath. If this were the case, I would much rather run than be dragged. In such a metaphysics, the primary pathways of existence would be engraved long before on the alter of existence, beyond the reach of our potency, but we may perhaps acquiesce to the chamber, skipping a crack in the floor here, pausing to view a etching there, all the while centrifugally being flung to and fro along our inevitable course. Here an inquisitive young philosopher might question who indeed was the architect of the chamber, a very impudent and proper question.

Closely related to the doctrine of Logos, and perhaps a subset of it, is the idea of True Will. The situation is similar to that presented above, and I am inclined to believe, an expansion of it. Pre-incarnation True Will has a great deal of determinism inherent in it; with the condolence being that fate is determined by self. The major difference between True Will and Logos is that Logos has the omnibalance as the primary matter of execution, whereas True Will aligns a course for the development and advancement of self, although even then it is guided by the auspices of the universe. The two doctrines become homogenous when it is understood that the universe sets broad parameters from within which the True Will is allowed to operate. In turn, in a man of gnosis, the True Will sets somewhat narrower parameters within which the ego operates. When the ego operates within these parameters, the soul is in harmony with the universe.

So herein is the optimal solution for that ancient question that plagues mankind, and for which an even more ancient mankind had the answer, being: how should I live my life? The wise determine their path and devote their full attention to it. All that we are made for, the questions of our purpose is summed up quite tidily: we are to do what we were made for; to do otherwise is to invite disaster.

Holding to the doctrine of pure Logos, one will simply be dragged miserable along one's course. In the case of True Will, one will simply fumble through and be ineffective and unhappy. Those hair-splitters, the profane who chose to heap dung upon the alters of the sacred by the audacity of calling themselves philosophers might like to point to this difference and guffaw in all of their so-called logic. Something is rotten in Denmark. But I shall extinguish the fiery logic of hair-splitting through urethral methodology. We must either ambulate upon our path with veracity or suffer the slings and arrows of outrageous fortune; the thousand natural shocks that flesh is heir to. He should have slain Claudius when he had the chance.

But to determine this purpose? One must turn eternally inward, shedding the false outward layers and gaining ever on that veritable center point of self. It is a very quiet voice that requires patience, solitude and quiet in order to perceive its atomic whispers.

In many ways our purpose snatches us up and hammers us upon the cosmic anvil. Then we are thrust into the coals. Ah, although the heat does burn; it is necessary for us to gain the malleability implicit in the forging; and then into the cool water, pleasurable and peaceful as the chill causes contraction and static stability, a consolidation of dynamics. But soon the soul will return to the fire once again, into the fiery chaos of change. Thus is the operation upon the soul, the path by which we shall eventually become the ultimate specialists as priests of the self. Just as a tool is engineered for a singular purpose, we each are to do what only we can: fulfill our role in the universe. Indeed, every man and woman is a star. We are priests in that we each form our own theology and ethics without need of intermediaries. Our Theology is the field manual that must be followed in order to harmonize with universal law. Some people's religion might be quite simply to treat others as you would be treated. Others might be far more complex with varying actions based on different circumstances. All ships may sail from different ports, but they will all reach the sea.

But you must not forget your purpose! All other crapulence must be thrown aside. Life is short, so you must focus to atomic diameter. We are each here to strike a pose in

An Account of the Holy Guardian Angel

the comedy of Pan, so there is no sense in spilling Chronos with distractions. They are just like a drug. They may offer a temporary satisfaction but in the end you just end up worse and less fit for the job.

A stultified conformist might ask why he should be concerned with fulfilling his purpose, even to the point of foregoing earthly pleasure. He might proceed to intone, quite slowly, mind you: "Why not just live life and enjoy?" Because true enjoyment is impossible without spiritual peace, with the gnawing maggots of doubt and the flies of nihilism feasting upon the cornucopia of our souls. Because all fickle pleasure is transitory and illusory. This "happiness" will soon come crashing down and the fool will find himself in the position of Job, scrapping at his proverbial sores with proverbial pottery shards, only without the benefit of faith because of his soul's neglect. A far greater number of rich and "successful" (whatever the hell that's supposed to mean) people commit suicide than poor people. The reason is that many poor people think that if they get a little more then they will be happy, but the rich have found out this isn't true and rather than face their disillusionment, they consign themselves to oblivion.

Not only for the reasons above should one follow their purpose, but also because there is a great joy in doing so, like a carpenter who is proud of what he has constructed. A hammer drives nails much better than it paddles a boat; a man is much happier having sex than when being used as a footstool. So are these distractions when compared to our purpose. Logos is deeper than logic.

Not long ago, I had an experience that parallels closely with the topic at hand. I had been out of work and had submitted my resume to a number of companies. I had been called up for a position as an assistant manager in a restaurant. I was doing it solely out of pecuniary concerns. I was sitting in the parking lot of the restaurant and suddenly I felt my insides gush out upon the hot pavement. I felt as though I were selling out and betraying myself. I was feeling very conflicted when a quiet voice told me to go to the bookstore. I wasn't sure about this course of action, but I followed through with it.

As soon as I walked in the door I saw the meditations of Marcus Aurelius. I immediately picked it up. After reading awhile I discovered a number of razors slicing into the scented mists of consciousness. It was not by mere chance that I saw this book. It was as if a curtain had been lifted as the room filled with a divine light that flooded my sentience, solving the many perplexities that I had been struggling with. It was at that moment that I realized (or perhaps re-realized, since I am not certain whether I was previously aware of it) that my life was not chaos.

I became sensitive to an unseen hand that was at that very moment guiding me, even as my surroundings dulled while retreating into peripheral consciousness. I then realized that this hand did not force my actions, but deftly unlocked doors that I was destined to move through. The numerous shattered fragments of identity coalesced into a stronger whole, which was far greater than the sum of its parts. Given the momentary glimpse of life, I realized then the dark shadow of futility inevitable in taking actions that conflict with my being. I knew that I had to penetrate through the walls of restriction toward the magnetic pull of my desire, which is not to be confused with those base and mundane needs that the body and mind had burdened me with; but rather the higher calling and sublime destiny that I knew of all along even though at times I was blinded from or away from which I foolishly turned my eyes, namely that of the True Will.

It should never be forgotten, that sacred duty of the initiate, to interpret all occurrences as the universe's particular dealing with one's soul. And on that day, as I took my new found treasure to the counter to pay, I heard once again the breathy whispers upon my ear. I was instructed to turn my gaze forthwith to a small stand. Upon looking, and seeing a collection of bookmarks, I hastily enveloped one into my appendage for closer inspection. Engraved upon the metal of the marker were the words: "Go

confidently in the direction of your dreams - H.D. Thoreau."
Like a small message in a fortune cookie, only with much
greater significance and cutting me much deeper, I felt as
though my soul had been cloven by a lighting bolt. There, in
a bookstore in the middle of the city, with the rumble of
thunder receding from my ears, I beheld both greatness and
destiny. It was there that I discovered truth on a simple
bookmark, not in the depths of a sylvan environment or a
hermit's solitude. The potency that had once tugged me
along the threads of destiny was upon me once again, and it
was proving a point so simple that I should have known all
along: it is not location that determines illumination, for all
location is but illusory.

The power also demonstrated that I was looking but
not trusting. I had been about to take a wrong path in life,
and I was humbly rebuked. But the power was not finished
with me yet. Let me now call this power my HGA. When I
was checking out, the pert girl was ringing up my items and
something started beeping. She looked slightly confused
and called another girl over. Between the two of them, they
finally were able to put an end to the beeping. The girl
looked back at me smiling and told me my total, which
seemed unusually low. I said nothing and handed her the
requested amount. As I walked away from the counter I
looked at my receipt: she had only charged me for the
bookmark, I had received the book for free. My HGA was
proving yet another point. When I follow his lead, events
will go well for me.

Here I would like to address the terms True Will and
HGA. They are both acceptable and they mean the same
thing. However, there is a danger in the term True Will. It
is easy, in fact far too easy, to shift from True Will to the ego,
and call your own desires your "True Will." It is here that a
person can get drawn into the vortex of ego, while losing
sight of the True Will, all the time unaware of the subtle
decline. That is what had happened to me; thus at that time
I had become a fallen priest. It is far too common to begin
attributing all sorts of things to the True Will when in fact

they are no such things. It all is related to the nature of Maya, and the internal and external messages.

The idea of Maya is that the world is illusionary, an idea I agree with. So, following such, where do the things of this world come from? It would have to be from the deeper recesses of the mind that we do not normally access. So if the actions of this world are messages, then they are messages coming from deep within, in other words, from the HGA.

Now, it is possible to receive messages from within. Of that there is no question. From whence do these communications originate? From the HGA or the ego? It is difficult, at least for me, to distinguish the difference at times. But with occurrences external there can be no doubt. I hear the squeak of objection here. Some might think that I am suggesting that a person walk through life, and when one approaches a crossroads flip a coin to see which direction to take. Damnable fools! I despise such chaos and have no wish to let the whore lady luck determine my destiny upon her whim. Everything that occurs must be filtered. Everything comes from a projection of the mind. But these images must be probed like the picture on a tarot card. You have to look for meaning. This is the job of the ego. The messages of the HGA are a guide, not a chain of servitude.

So it was that these realizations came to me while standing in the bookstore. But even this was not yet the extent of what was revealed to me during my communication with my Holy Guardian Angel.

After receiving this weighty revelation, I didn't feel like driving. I told my soul mate Katherine that I was not yet ready to leave, that I wanted to get some coffee. She merely shrugged at me and gave me one of those looks when she thinks I'm acting weird. As she drifted off to look at magazines, I did indeed get myself a large coffee, and then stretched out in a black leather chair to meditate. I sat there for a while, staring at the steam rise slowly from the hot

An Account of the Holy Guardian Angel

coffee in my hand, becoming oblivious to my surroundings. The entire experience had struck me a starting blow.

For some time I had been drifting along life, what might be called traveling laterally. Until that day I had felt a total desolation at my lack of purpose. I knew that I had lost my True Will, that I had lost conversation with my HGA. Hard as I tried, I could formulate exactly no meaning to my existence, and considered my life to be one of complete failure. But as I sat in that chair sipping on my coffee, the black tendrils of nihilism slowly began to uncoil themselves from around my soul, and then made a quick retreat from the light I then noticed forming in my immediate vicinity. The veil had been torn asunder.

I began to understand that my HGA was not always with me; at least as far as waking consciousness was concerned. His presence is sometimes strong, but at times faint. I then realized that when in his presence, I had better give my full attention. That is exactly what I did on that fateful afternoon and the results were extraordinary.

I heard a voice once again, and with its inception, the room fell away like so many leaves in fall, and I heard nothing but His voice, and beheld nothing but His terrible presence. A voice like thunder ran towards me.

"If you were rich and could do anything you pleased, what would you do?"

I was ready and I told the Mighty One that I would be a philosopher and spiritual teacher, and that I would write. Without pause, He responded.

"Then why aren't you doing it?" the voice rolled in return, washing over my being and assaulting me both with its potency and by the way it had stripped me naked and removed all my pretensions. I stuttered and attempted to offer feeble excuses about the expectations of others and the difficulties of doing such things. As I spoke the words, I could see tiny glass spheres containing visualizations of my excuses, realizing as I saw them before me how low and cowardly they were. My Holy Guardian Angel took the small globes, which he gleefully smashed whist laughing at me. Of course I did not get angry with Him, rather I felt abashed at His scolding. I realized that He had released me from chains by which I had voluntarily shackled myself.

But first, I wish to emphasize that it was at that moment that my HGA smashed all of my pathetic illusions I had built up around myself. I had realized my path. It was obvious, but the dirty illusions had smeared my vision. He had been trying to tell me, but I was too far away and did not hear.

I had thought that I had reached the peak of the mountain; that I had ascended to complete enlightenment and had reached the end of my journey. I had then lost sight of the Prince. The Prince looked to these others who had placed silver leashes around my neck, those who lead me so carefully this way and that, gently nudging me out of my orbit. These He scoffed at and called them "gaping fools who cannot even order their own lives, much less give direction to others. There is only one light. I am the light. These who would advise you do not have the first inkling concerning the mechanisms which order the universe."

The Angel is infallible, eternal, everything. I was only a mortal and a shell of ignorance. That peak I was standing on was only a foothill at the edge of the mountain. And while I had been busy shaking my own hand, I was in my egotism blind to the glory of the peak before me, and of the Angel who had trodden steadily on the path upward. I had become lost because I failed to hear his warnings, did not see him as he pointed to the mountain, so that He finally had to climb back down to retrieve me, and what a sorry shape He found me in! There, curled in a fetal position cold and hungry, and wondering why I felt so bad now that I had reached the summit. My Angel is a harsh teacher.

"Better keep up," He told me before, "because if you fall behind you will be in sorry shape."

When He did find me, I was in the restaurant parking lot, feeling confused and miserable. He did not wrap his wings around me and comfort me for my transgressions. Instead he picked me up and smacked me

An Account of the Holy Guardian Angel

smartly across the face. Once He had knocked me out of my ego-driven daze He said, "Wake up you idiot, the mountain is over there." Then he pointed.

As I looked upward at the enormous peak I was then the gaping fool. I was standing on the ant-hill. Oh foolish pride and deceptive arrogance. What an evil bitch she is! So thus is the account of my Angel smashing all of my illusions and raking away all the small stickmen, which I had been listening to. He destroyed them all. And in his power and glory his left hand was empty; yea it was empty. Amen.

The Star Sapphire

The Way to Suceed-

Plunge from the height, O God,
and interlock with Man!

Plunge from the height, O Man,
and interlock with Beast!

    The Star Sapphire is principally a sexual ritual. This may not come as a shock to some, and to others it may be new information. The ritual exudes sexuality to be sure, but my point is that Crowley intended sex to actually play a part in the ritual. The reason he did not say so more explicitly has much to do with the time period it was written in.

The Star Sapphire

Firstly, the two interlocking hexagrams are very indicative of the sexual act. This ritual represents sex in both symbolism and practice. It can be performed without a physical sexual element, although I think perhaps it is less powerful. I hope to incorporate and translate my findings for a complete understanding of the ritual.

In the instructions the Magick Rood is the phallus and the Mystic Rose is the yoni. The formulation of the Hexagrams proceeds as stated. After this, the formulation of the "Rosy Cross," which even Crowley put into parenthesis, is the sexual act. This is done while repeating the mantra: Ararita over and over. Ararita is of course Notariqon of Hebrew which translates, "One is His Beginning; One is His Individuality; His Permutation One." Crowley states that "ARARITA is a formula of the Macrocosm potent in certain very lofty operations of the Magick of the Inmost Light."[84]

In *The Book of Lies* is hidden many references to Crowley's work, in a plain but disguised form. The object was that those who pursued the knowledge of working things out were worthy to receive the methods. Chapter 36 gives the Star Sapphire itself, but leave it to Crowley's humor to put the rest of the equation in Chapter 69.

The title is "The Way to Succeed- and the way to suck eggs!" In the commentary, Crowley states that "The key to the understanding of this chapter is given in the number and the title, the former being intelligible to all nations who employ Arabic figures, the latter only to experts in deciphering English puns."[85] The 69 of the chapter is indeed a reference to the double oral sexual act, and the "sucking eggs" a subtle reference of the priest drawing out the female sexual fluids, which in *De Arte Magica* he refers to as the "Gluten." I don't think that the 69 method is the only way in which the sexual unification can be performed, however.

---

[84] Crowley, *Magick*, 168.
[85] Crowley, *Lies*, 148-49.

Musings of a Thelemite

The primary purpose of the Star Sapphire is a uniting of opposites, as is hinted in the 5=6. The act itself should be a uniting of the priest who has invoked Set with his virgin sacrifice, as well as a uniting of the priest with God. This then makes clear the passage in the ritual which reads, "Also shall Set appear in the Circle."[86] Looking down, the priest is God and the virgin the daughter or Malkuth. Looking up, the priest is the daughter calling to unification, and he must sacrifice himself for that unity. As above so below. The symbolism in the ritual is absolutely astounding, which is further hinted at in chapter 69:

> This is the Holy Hexagram.
> Plunge from the height, O God, and interlock with Man!
> Plunge from the height, O Man, and interlock with Beast!

Here is the magician made Tiphareth, pinned between Kether and Malkuth. He must reflect what is above to down below. This idea is linked with the word ABRAHADABRA, which is appropriate since it is an interlocked word, with 5 letters identical and 6 different, thus representing the 5=6, and the obtainment of the Holy Guardian Angel, which is also symbolized by the interlocking of the two triangles of the hexagram. This also represents the interlocking of the male principle [6] and the female principle [5]. The red triangle pointing downward is the fire of Horus, and the blue upward triangle is supplications rising to heaven.

It is in *De Arte Magica* that Crowley gives the practical workings of sexual magic. This book was taken off the market by the OTO, for whatever reasons. The first sentence reads, "The supreme secret of the O.T.O. [sex magick] is written in detail in the Book called Agape and is also written plainly in Liber CCCXXXIII, Cap. XXXVI." The second reference is of course to the Star Sapphire.

---

[86] Ibid., 82.

90

The Star Sapphire

There is a great amount of symbolic language in this text, after the fashion of alchemy. *De Arte Magica* makes it quite clear that the sacrament, or semen, of the operation is to be consumed. Crowley states, "It is said by the O.H.O. that of this perfect medicine a single dewdrop sufficeth, and this may be true. Yet it is humbly and with all deference and worship Our opinion that every drop generated (so far as may be possible) should be consumed." This concept is reflected in the Star Sapphire ritual, as it states, "Let him drink of the Sacrament and let him communicate the same." Again is this injunction repeated in the 69th chapter: "This Work also eats up itself, accomplishes its own end, nourishes the worker, leaves no seed, is perfect in itself."

Crowley does a good job of answering in his opinion the sub-questions that may arise while practicing these operations as well in *De Arte Magica*. He makes clear that during orgasm and the consumption of the sacrament, the priest must be fully focused on the object of his operation. In the case of the Star Sapphire, the visual focus is the hexagram, and the verbal (if desired) would be Ararita.

He also deals with the question of anal sex for the operation, humorously calling it the "Nuptial of the Folk of Earth." Make note that this is not necessarily homosexual, as is often alleged, when people refer to the "secret XI degree," as it refers to the XI chapter of the text. He does state that in the "Earth" operation, the "Sacrament cannot exist, for that there is no White Eagle to generate the Gluten." He states that the earth ritual is for other purposes. Since it does not generate the sacrament, it would not seem to be a viable method for the Star Sapphire.

De Arte Magicka is a very useful text, and I would like to see it republished. The reason for the coded language was both to protect his oaths and because of the censorship of the times. Ironically enough, he offers a great deal of magical advice in a very straightforward way, once the "code" is understood. Much of it could be applied to non-magical operations.

The Development of Kabbala

The Development of Kabbala

The Kabbala is a way of thought that originally came from the Hebrew people, however not all Jews are Kabbalists; neither are all Kabbalists Jews. It is a very complex system that has its roots at least in the first century, if not before. Unfortunately, the sands of time have mostly buried the Kabbala from common knowledge. The Kabbala contains within it a foundational structure that can answer the questions of philosophers, psychologists and theologians, as well as giving a person peace and a path to enlightenment. Within the structure of the Kabbala is the ability to harmonize opposing schools of thought, to see them in relation to each other; most substantially in the case of science and religion. Kabbalist Aleister Crowley's life work was "to synthesize the aim of religion and the method of science."[87]

The Kabbala is not a book, religion, or creed. There is no one book called "The Kabbala," although there are numerous writings that can be termed Kabbalistic. It is a way of looking at the world, at God, and at humanity. The term Kabbala comes from a Hebrew word which means "to receive."[88] There are no authorities on the Kabbala, and each person discovers for himself what truth means and how he stands with God. It is a very personal thing, and in a way, every student has his own Kabbala. Every student must "receive" truth from God in his own way. At the very heart of Kabbala is the Tree of Life, which I will explain in greater detail later.

The ancient Hebrews had three sacred sets of texts: the Torah, the Talmud, and the Kabbala. The Torah equates with the first five books of the Old Testament, said to have been written by Moses. The Talmud was a rabbinic commentary written on the Torah. The Kabbala was a collection of writings and an oral tradition that dealt with mystical interpretations about God and the universe. The

---

[87] Eshelman, *Mystical & Magical System*, 13.
[88] Regardie, *Garden*, 3.

Hebrews once said that if an ignorant man studied the Torah, then he would live a better life; the learned man should study the Talmud to gain knowledge; and those who were wise should meditate upon the Kabbala.[89]

Kabbalistic methods help to awaken the consciousness and let one unite and commune with God. My friend and fellow student once told me: "The goal of our existence is to become enlightened, and the Kabbala is the tool. If you don't realize the goal, then the Kabbala is meaningless." The Kabbala is the ancient spiritual underpinning of both Judaism and Christianity. It has never been completely one with either of them, however. It encourages a student to think for himself and to discover truth by experimentation. It is essentially a system of mysticism, but does contain a great amount of scholarship and intellectual work that would belie any attempt to put Kabbala along side New Age feel-good religions that have sprouted up in the past few years.

The Kabbala shows you the path, so that you may receive the knowledge for yourself, rather than supplying the answers. It is not complicated in its quintessence. Regardie says the Kabbala is so simple "that a vast amount of self-discipline and training is required to make it effective."[90] The truth is not complicated, but the methods for perfecting the soul are not always easy. It is a system of doing, of contemplating.

According to Jewish legend, the Kabbala was given to Adam by an angel after he and Eve were cast out of the Garden of Eden, so that man might find his way back to God once again. The story tells of how humanity turned its collective back on God, and the great deluge came. After the flood was over, God gave Noah the secret teachings of Kabbala once again. Later it would be given to Moses when he spent forty days on top of Mount Sinai. When he saw the idol worship of the people he destroyed these secrets and

[89] Kraig, *Modern Magick*, 52.
[90] Regardie, *Introduction*, 3.

returned to the mountain. He then received the Ten Commandments, which represented legalism. Apparently the mass of Hebrew people was not yet ready for the responsibility and freedom that Kabbala entailed. God told Moses that the secrets of the Kabbala were to be kept by Aaron and the future high priests, for the common man could not be trusted with them.[91]

Of the various texts written on Kabbala, two in particular stand out. The first book is called the Sepher ha-Zohar "Book of Splendor" and the second is the Sepher Yetzirah "Book of Formation." Noted hermetic scholar William Westcott was the first to translate the Sepher Yetzirah into English, in 1887. In his introduction, he wrote that the Sepher Yetzirah "is not in any sense a narrative of Creation, or a substitute Genesis, but is an ancient and instructive philosophical treatise upon one aspect of the origin of the universe and mankind; an aspect at once archaic and essentially Hebrew."[92] Essentially, the Sepher Yetzirah details how God created the universe through the twenty-two letters of the Hebrew alphabet. It is written in very vague language, and represents a very primitive Kabbala, which the Rabbis were to later transform into a much more sophisticated system.

Another towering figure in Kabbala scholarship is Gershom Scholem, who became Professor of Mysticism and Kabbala at Hebrew University, Jerusalem. Scholem is perhaps the best source concerning the historical development of the Kabbala. Pertaining to the Sepher Yetzirah, he concluded that it was "the earliest extant Hebrew text of systematic, speculative thought," and a "compact discourse on cosmology and cosmogony." Scholem estimates that the book was composed between the third and sixth centuries.[93] The text places great significance on the three Hebrew mother letters: aleph, mem, and shin,

---

[91] Kraig, *Modern Magick*, 54.
[92] Westcott, *Sepher Yetzirah*.
[93] Scholem, *Kabbalah*, 23-27.

which represent the three elements of air, water, and fire, respectively. From these, everything else came into being.

There were strong Kabbalistic movements in France, Germany, Egypt, and Spain during the Middle Ages. Moses de Leon, a Spanish Jew, wrote the Zohar around 1280. The Zohar examines the nature of the Sephiroth in detail, which became the fundamental aspect of Kabbala. Although antedating the Zohar, Fig. 1 shows how Medieval Kabbalists conceptualized The Tree of Life and the Sephiroth.[94] The Sephiroth are the division of the universe into certain archetypes, which will be examined in detail below. Leon examined these archetypes and how they related to symbols that can be seen in everyday life. He stressed that only through a mystical understanding of Kabbala, and of these Sephiroth could Jews fully appreciate and understand the Torah.[95]

---

[94] Fig. 1 was originally the title page of Portae Lucis, a Latin translation by Paulus Ricius of J. Gikatilla, Sha'arei Orah, Augsburg, 1516.
[95] Scholem, *Kabbalah*, 23-27.

Figure 1. An early depiction of The Tree of Life.

After the Zohar, the next major evolution of Kabbala came about by a man named Isaac Luria (1534-72). Luria, who was heavily influenced by Gnostic sources, greatly systemized the Kabbala into methods for obtaining communion with God. Luria stressed meditation and mystical prayer in such a way that echoed the techniques of yoga in the east. These teachings spread among Jews and caused a great spiritual evolution among its practitioners. Kabbala began to be accepted among mainstream lines. Along with this systematic mysticism was a strong messianic element among his followers. They believed him to be a messiah of Joseph who would pave the way for the greater messiah of David. Unknown to them, this seed in many ways planted the downfall of Kabbalism within mainstream Judaic thought.[96]

During the early seventeenth century arose a Jew named Sabbatai Zvi, who is perhaps one of the most bizarre figures in history. At an early age Zvi took to the Kabbala, especially the system of Isaac Luria. In line with custom, he married early, but avoided intercourse with his wife, which lead to their divorce. The scenario was repeated with a second wife. He became stricter upon himself, bathing in the sea, even in winter; fasted day after day, and lived constantly in a state of ecstasy.

During this time there was a great deal of millenarianism among both Jews and Christians. Many Christian writers placed 1666 as the year of the apocalypse. Then certain Jews made a computation based on a passage in the Zohar, and decided that in 1648 Israel would be redeemed by the Messiah. In 1648, at the age of twenty two, Zvi revealed himself to be the long awaited Messiah to a band of followers in Smyrna, claiming that he would "overthrow the governments," and "restore Israel to Jerusalem." It was shortly after this that he was thrown out of the city by the local Rabbis. In Salonica, he celebrated his marriage to the Torah, which caused him to be banished from this city as well.

He traveled around continuing to proclaim himself as the Messiah, forging "ancient" documents that predicted his name and birth. He made believers out of many wealthy Jews, which helped to finance his cause. Despite the dubious methods of his publicity campaign, his popularity continued to grow with both Jews and Christians. His fame and followers spread throughout Europe, and even far-away Holland had centers of Messianic activity. Fantastic stories began to spread through these centers; for instance it was

---

[96] Ibid., 74-76.

98

said that a ship had appeared north of Scotland with silken sails and ropes, manned by sailors who spoke Hebrew. The flag bore the inscription 'The Twelfe Tribes of Israel.'

In the prophetic year of 1666, Zvi headed for Constantinople, hoping that a miracle would happen. As he stepped off his ship he was immediately arrested and thrown into prison. He soon secured a great leniency due to bribes from his rich followers. His arrest, rather than slowing the Messianic movement, caused it to reach extreme levels, partly due to the miraculous deeds that he was supposedly performing there. In parts of Europe, Jews began to unroof their houses and prepare for the exodus. Zvi's initials were posted in synagogues and prayer-books were issued containing his picture.

Things went from bad to worse for Zvi when Sultan Mohammed IV learned of treasonable plans that Zvi had been scheming. The sultan's physician advised Zvi to convert to Islam as the only method of saving his life. When Zvi was brought before the sultan the next day, he cast off his Jewish garb and put a Turkish turban on his head; and thus his conversion to Islam was accomplished. Many of Zvi's followers joined him in the conversion. Zvi then took a slave as second wife. He released a pronouncement to the Jews of the world: "God has made me an Ishmaelite; He commanded, and it was done. The ninth day of my regeneration." The sultan was pleased with this and made him a free man with a position in his court along with a substantial salary.

Confusion set in among the expectant Jews everywhere. To make matters worse, Muslims and Christians jeered at and scorned the credulous and duped Jews. Zvi then began playing both sides. Among Muslims he would revile Judaism; among Jews he would do the opposite. He then published a manifesto to the Jews declaring that he was the Messiah, with the aim being to convert thousands of Muslims to Judaism. When the sultan questioned his activity, he told him that it was just a ruse to convert the Jews to Islam. The result of this and other activities was that he converted a number of Muslims into Islamic Kabbalists, but then brought many Jews to Islam. Soon enough the sultan tired of his schemes and banished him to a small place in Albania, where he died in loneliness and obscurity.

Those conservative Kabbalists who were never caught up in Sabbatan movement decided from then on to restrict the Kabbala for the elite few, to preserve the stability of Judaism from the rabid mobs of messianic followers. These Rabbis returned to the Kabbala of Luria, and continued their work in a very esoteric spirit from 1700 onward and kept their activities mostly hidden.[97]

Due to the secretive nature of the Kabbalists, the number of Kabbalistic books available in English was fairly limited. It was the Hermetics who first began the translation of texts. A lot of information was brought to light during the Victorian Age in Great Britain and France. It was during that time that Westcott translated portions of the Zohar, and A. E. Waite made summaries of important Kabbalistic works during this era.[98] Coming into the early twentieth century, both Aleister Crowley and Israel Regardie made many philosophic and practical writings that bring the Kabbala to light.

Aleister Crowley is a name that is almost universally despised by those that know him, although not entirely fairly. He was hated by other Hermeticists, particularly the "Hermetic Order of the Golden Dawn," because he couldn't bear their secrecy, and so published their esoteric and Kabbalistic information for all to benefit from. He was hated by his contemporary Victorians because his lifestyle was contrary to the morals of the time. He continues to be hated by Kosher Kabbalists today because he intermingled the Kabbala with outside sources, including Taoism, Buddhism, Tantra, Yoga, alchemy, and mythology. This position is particularly interesting considering that the Kabbala can

---

[97] Ibid., 80.
[98] Regardie, *Garden*, 12.

hardly be considered strictly Jewish in any sense. Its entire historical development shows it to be a syncretic work combining elements of Sufism, Gnosticism, Christian asceticism, and Neo-Platonism among other sources.

Crowley died in 1947, but recently his books have enjoyed a resurgence of interest. It is interesting to note that after his books began to be seen on shelves again, there has been a prolific outpouring of kosher books from Jews who wish to counter his influence. A typical kosher opinion can be seen of Scholem, who remarked of Crowley and other Hermetics in passing fashion:

> [They] lacked any basic knowledge of the sources and very rarely contributed to the field, while at times they even hindered the development of a historical approach...The activities of French and English occultists contributed nothing and only served to create considerable confusions between the teachings of the Kabbalah and their own totally unrelated inventions.[99]

Although it might be easy to dismiss Crowley as an "occultist," he was far from the superstitious ignoramus that Scholem paints him to be. It is important to establish this if we are to put faith in Crowley's work and thought. Crowley was an educated man, attended Cambridge University, was an accomplished etymologist, knew French, German, Latin, Greek, Hebrew, Russian, and to some extent Aramaic, Egyptian Hieroglyphs and Chinese. He was a gifted poet, and although perhaps not as well known as some, is included in certain Oxford anthologies to this day. In his writings he demonstrates a deep knowledge of both western and eastern philosophy, and an intimacy with various mythologies. He both understood and took part in scientific research of his time. He was for a time a chess master, beating almost all champions of England and Scotland, but decided it was a waste of time and gave it up. He was also a mountain climber, and succeeded in breaking many records

---

[99] Scholem, *Kabbalah*, 203.

on the peaks of the Himalayas. He studied hermetic magic in England, yoga in India, Buddhism in Ceylon, and Sufism in Egypt, all in his quest for enlightenment. Probably the twentieth-century's greatest unknown genius, he was almost universally misunderstood by his contemporaries and continues to be largely misunderstood and ignored today.

Both Scholem and Crowley are very useful to a study of Kabbala. Scholem is a masterful, careful historian of the evolution of Kabbala, and is invaluable to a historical study of the field. But Crowley is a man who took Kabbala, as well as other systems, and walked where angels fear to tread. For Scholem it was an intellectual passion and he received his information from history, for Crowley it was a means of truth and salvation, and he never needed to look outside of himself for the answer. By using both of these minds we can see both sides and therefore gain a complete understanding of Kabbala.

Thus there is what could be called two Kabbalas. The first is the Kosher Kabbala and the second is the Hermetic Kabbala. At heart, these are both the same system, just with different applications; however there is often a great animosity felt toward the Hermetic Kabbala by more orthodox Jews, who sometimes refer to it as the WASP Kabbala in derision. Originally there was only Kosher Kabbala, which is the traditional Kabbala. The Hermetic Kabbala came about from non-Jews such as Crowley who saw the strength of the system, but shared a different background. So they adopted it to their understanding by infusing Greek, Egyptian, and other systems into it. And for a non-Jew it makes the system much more intelligible. One does not need years of Jewish background in order to comprehend the ideas in the Hermetic Kabbala. Hermetic Kabbala also does not presuppose knowledge of Hebrew, although study of the language is necessary in order to understand some of the deeper applications.

If I explained that the Sephira Geburah could be understood by its relation to Ares, the Greek god of war, then this would be intelligible since it is a prominent aspect of western civilization. Much more so than if I gave the kosher explanation of the god-name, Eloheem-Giboor, or that the archangel was Khamael who ruled over the Serapheem. The Kosher Kabbala is an amazing source of information and understanding, and students of the Hermetic Kabbala will eventually drift over to it at least in part.

The central figure for every Kabbalist is the Tree of life. This symbol contains hidden references that unite the world's religions as a useable whole. It shows the harmony underlying all religious systems of the world, and how one can study various spiritual teachers without conflict. The sum total of all knowledge and experience, whether religious, philosophical, or scientific, can be found in the Tree of Life. It unites everything in the entire universe into thirty-two sections. Fig. 2 shows an illustration of the Tree of Life. The ten circles are the Sephiroth, which basically means "emanation" in Hebrew. Each title is shown in Table 1. Sephiroth is plural and Sephira is the singular. Numbered eleven through thirty-two are the paths, which correspond to the twenty-two letters of the Hebrew alphabet. There is not space in an essay of this sort to fully detail out the significance of each path, so I will restrict myself primarily to the discussion of the Sephiroth.

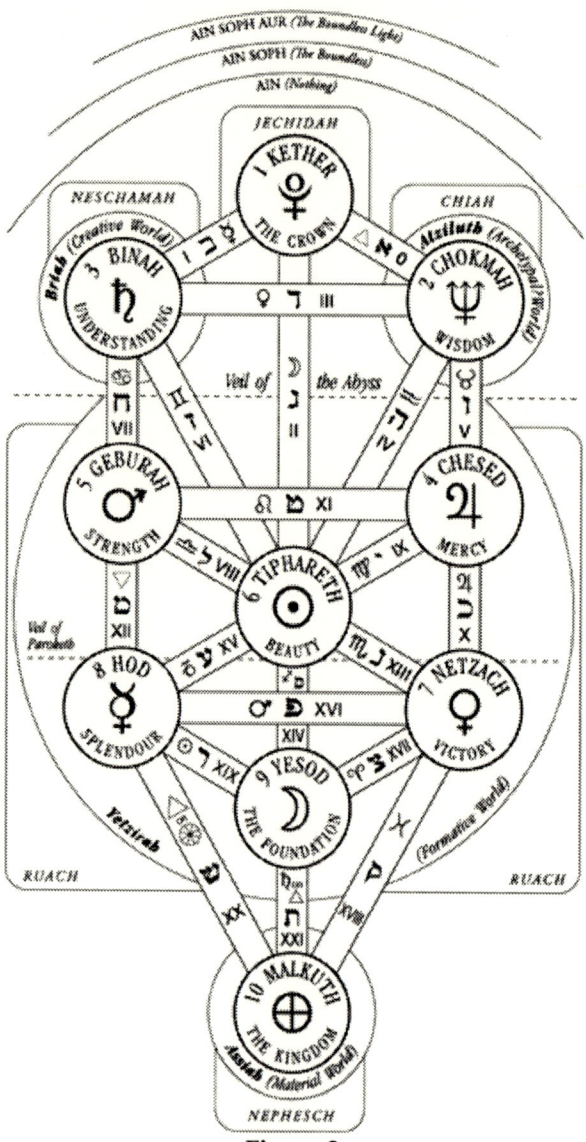

Figure 2
The Tree of Life.

The Development of Kabbala

Table 1
Titles of the Sephiroth

1. Kether (Crown)

2. Chokmah (Wisdom)

3. Binah (Understanding)

4. Chesed (Mercy)

5. Geburah (Strength)

6. Tiphareth (Beauty)

7. Netzach (Victory)

8. Hod (Glory)

9. Yesod (Foundation)

10. Malkuth (Kingdom)

The numeration of the Sephiroth and paths are very important, as each number holds a particular meaning which can illuminate further mysteries later on. First an examination of the tree will be made from the bottom upward, in terms of advancing consciousness. This is one of the many ways in which this symbol can be used. Malkuth – 10 is the lower-most Sephira. Malkuth means "kingdom" and corresponds to what we would recognize as physical reality. Pythagoras thought that ten was the most complete number because 1+2+3+4=10.This is the place of cold matter. It is where our bodies exist, but not our minds or souls. It contains everything that registers on our five senses.

The first step upward is to Yesod-9, which means "foundation." Yesod is the place of dreaming and the unconscious mind. This is the easiest level to access above Malkuth. In Hermetic Kabbala, Yesod would also correspond to activities such as divination, telepathy, astral travel and Hatha Yoga. The reason that Yesod is called the foundation is because it is the place of spiritual reality, so-called. It holds the spiritual or astral forms that create a basis for physical reality, such as it is. To think that the spirit world of Yesod is a reflection or shadow of Malkuth is incorrect Kabbala. Malkuth is really a shadow of Yesod. It is the reality in Yesod that gives us physical reality. If it is so in Yesod, then it shall be so in Malkuth. Herein was a secret of the Kabbalists. If one could make changes in Yesod, then it would be so on Malkuth.

It is important to point out at this time that the Sephiroth should not be thought of merely in terms of magical abilities or powers. It is true that the ancient Jews used Kabbala in methods that might be categorized as "magic," and many make use of that aspect today, but that word has connotations that skew the real significance. One of the main uses of the Tree of Life is to categorize experience and reality. Furthermore, once the lower levels are bypassed, the Sephiroth become more and more abstract.

The next steps upon the Tree of Life are Netzach-7 and Hod-8. Netzach and Hod play off of each other in ways that Yesod and Malkuth do not. So it is best to consider them together. Netzach means victory. This is a sphere that can be related to hedonistic nature rites, such as was attributed to Pan. It is an area of passion and emotion. Arts, music, and all the Romantic elements are part of Netzach. The classical divinity of Netzach is Venus or Aphrodite. Conversely, Hod means glory and is a place of studious thought and study. It is the foundation for hermetic ritual magick. Here logic rules and the presiding deity is Mercury or Hermes. A study of mythology can be very useful in understanding divisions of reality. Indeed, the Greeks later viewed their gods more in terms of archetypes, as place holders for different concepts such as war, love and so on. It is exactly in such a way that the tree of life is used, but with the added significance of characterizing the varieties of consciousness. Netzach represents a path of enlightenment through ecstatic methods, such as dance, music, and drugs. Historically, the shaman of certain primitive tribes would follow these methods. On the other hand Hod is not tied up with emotion, but with intellect and reason. This is enlightenment through the contemplation of the philosopher.

In Nietzsche's *The Birth of Tragedy*, he spoke of the differences between the rites of Apollo and the rites of Dionysus, which align perfectly with the concepts here. The spirit of Apollo, and by extension Hod, is "individual, rational, and calm." Dionysus and Netzach are "communal, irrational, and frenzied."[100] Neither path or method of raising consciousness is considered to be superior to the other. As can be seen in Fig. 2, the Sephiroth are co-equal with each other.

Tiphareth-6 is the center of the tree, and the center of a person. It corresponds to the heart chakra and to the physical heart. It is the solar center. It is where the True Will is located, and in order for a person to find their true path in life, they must ascend the tree to at least this point. In many ways Tiphareth is the most important Sephira on the tree. In translation, it means simply "beauty." Jesus in particular gives a vivid example of Tiphareth, for to know the true self you must sacrifice all. Everything must be abandoned for the higher good, which is an extreme and difficult thing to do. Once the True Will is acquired, all doubt is erased, and all obstacles are brushed aside.

Moving on above Tiphareth are Chesed-4 and Geburah-5, which feed into Tiphareth. Like 7 & 8, these are opposing forces. Chesed is mercy and Geburah is strength. A good way to look at these two principles is with an example. If someone broke the law, and the judge wanted to be lenient, then he would be showing attributes of Chesed. If

---

[100] Nietzsche, *Birth of Tragedy*, 319.

on the other hand, he gave out a severe punishment to deter further crime, then Geburah would be the dominating force. In terms of mythology, Chesed is ruled by Zeus, the paternal king of the gods and Geburah is ruled by Ares, god of war. They are two sides of the same coin. They must be balanced in life in order to prosper. Too much mercy and a person will be overrun and taken advantage of; if an overly critical and judgmental approach is taken, then people will not tolerate it for long. Another way to see it is that Chesed is building up and Geburah is a tearing down. Both are necessary in order to accomplish anything. Chesed is trust, and Geburah is doubt.

Between Chesed-4 and Binah-3 is said to lay the abyss Da'ath. Da'ath is not a Sephira, but a place that separates the highest part of the Tree with the lower. The abyss "has no number, for in it all is confusion."[101] Once the abyss is crossed, then true spiritual understanding is complete. It is comparable to the ego destruction that is sought out by practitioners of Yoga or Buddhism.

Above the abyss, things are purely abstract. The uppermost three Sephiroth are called the supernal triad, and Crowley states that they are unity, "in a manner transcending reason. The comprehension of this Trinity is a matter of spiritual experience."[102] Binah is "understanding" and the dark mother principle. Chokmah means "wisdom" and is the fiery father figure. Chokmah is chaos and Binah is order. Above both of these is Kether, which means crown. Kether is the single divinity. There is little to be said about Kether. It is 1, undivided and indivisible. To begin to separate it so that it can be understood is to create the entire Tree of Life. All other Sephiroth proceed from Kether. In many senses, it can be thought of as God, "The Way" of the Taoists. When a Hindu is asked to define God he says, "Not that, not that," for to define is to limit and Kether is without limit.

---

[101] Crowley, *Magick*, 138.
[102] Ibid.

The Development of Kabbala

This outline of reality by the Kabbalists was influenced by I Chronicles 29:11, which clearly corresponds to the outline in the tree of life: "Thine, O Lord is the greatness, [Chesed 4] and the power, [Geburah 5] and the glory, [Hod 8] and the victory, [Netzach 7] and the majesty [uniting in Tiphareth 6]: for all that is in the heaven [Kether 1] and in the earth [Malkuth 10] is thine; thine is the kingdom, O Lord, and thou art exalted as head above all.

Looking at the tree from the bottom up, and as an evolution of consciousness is only one of the many ways that this symbolism can be viewed. Another method is to view the tree from Kether downward in terms of the method of creation. This idea of deriving many from one probably reflects the influence of Neo-Platonism during the development of Kabbala. Crowley illustrates this process in his book 777, as depicted in Table 2.[103]

---

[103] Crowly, 777, 28-29.

Table 2
Process of Creation

1. The Self of Deity, beyond Fatherhood and Motherhood.
2. The Father.
3. The Mother.
4. The Father made flesh- authoritative and paternal.
5. The Mother made flesh- fierce and active.
6. The Son- partaking of all these natures.
7. The Mother degraded to mere animal emotion.
8. The Father degraded to mere animal reason.
9. The Son degraded to mere animal life.
10. The Daughter, fallen and touching with her hands the shells.

Table 3
The Tree in the Microcosm

1. The Self- the divine Ego of which man is rarely conscious.
2. The Ego; that which thinks "I" – a falsehood, because to think "I" is to deny "not-I" and thus to create the Dyad [dualistic thinking, subject-object, etc.].
3. The Soul; since 3 reconciles 2 and 1, here are placed the aspirations to divinity. It is also the receptive as 2 is the assertive self.

4-9. The Intellectual Self, with its branches:
4. Memory.
5. Will.
6. Imagination.
7. Desire.
8. Reason.
9. Animal being.
6. The Conscious Self of the Normal Man: thinking itself free, and really the toy of its surroundings.
9. The Unconscious Self of the Normal Man. Reflex actions, circulation, breathing, digestion, etc., all pertain here.
10. The illusory physical envelope; the scaffolding of the building.

Here the progression is seen to degenerate, ending in the world as we know it. This is precisely the reason why the Kabbalist wishes to "climb back up the tree," as it were. Note that the daughter is touching "the shells." In Kabbalistic symbolism this refers to negative demonic influences that are below Malkuth.

Hermetic Kabbalists have a saying, "as above, so below," meaning that the microcosm is a reflection of the macrocosm. So as the Tree of Life reflects flow of cosmic forces, so does it divide a human being. Again, Crowley demonstrates the divisions in 777, as seen in Table 3.[104]

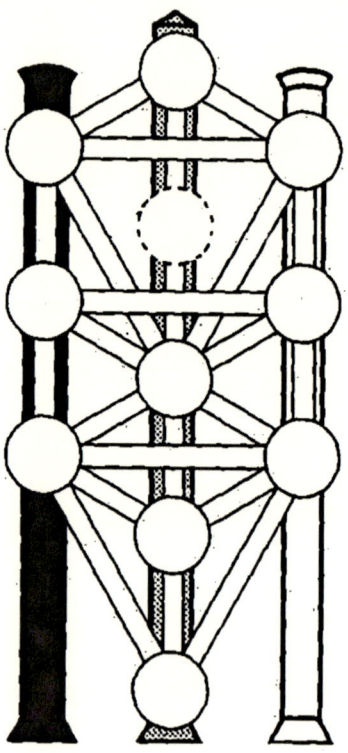

Figure 3
The Three Pillars

---

[104] Ibid.

The Development of Kabbala

Yet another way of looking at The Tree of Life is seeing it as three pillars, as is seen in Fig. 3. This view has at least some very ancient sources. It may be that the concept of the three pillars was conceived of before the diagram of the tree itself, and that the Sephiroth were then placed in such a way to make these two systems homogenous. There is evidence in this concept as far back as the Temple of Solomon. Although forbidden to raise any sort of idol, the Jews compromised by including two highly ornate pillars as part of the architecture. The right was called Jachin (He shall establish) and the left was Boaz (in it is strength).[105] The harmony between the right pillar and Chesed "Mercy" is obvious; thus the left pillar corresponds to Geburah "Strength." The right pillar has come to be called The Pillar of Mercy, the left The Pillar of Severity, which leaves in the center The Middle Pillar, which has also been called 'The Staff of Aaron.' The Middle Pillar is seen as the good life, the avoidance of extremes, which bares close similarity to Aristotle's 'middle way.' A Kabbalist tries to avoid an excess of mercy or severity, logic or emotion.

There really are no bounds to the methods of division, and the ways in which these symbols can be applied to various groups of ideas. Indeed, Kabbalists have spent centuries doing just that. This is the method of using the Tree of Life for contemplation by correspondence. Kabbalah, as a system, contains many other methods that grow in complexity beyond these simple divisions. The numerology, which in Kabbalah is called Gematria, goes beyond these ten or thirty-two divisions, and examines numbers stretching into the hundreds. Crowley's book 777 is primarily a book of numbers, and he worked with most numbers up to one thousand in relation with Kabbala. Kabbalists use this and other methods to gain deeper meaning from the ancient Hebrew texts, such as the Torah and Talmud.

---

[105] Gray, *Qabalistic Concepts*, 114.

Musings of a Thelemite

Although not an easy system to learn, but the art and science of using these divisions allows one to see differences between things, and the intricate connection of all things. Once the Tree of Life is finally planted into the mind, one will be able to classify any event, thought, or object into consciousness and see its relation to every other thought that has entered the mind. By this method, one's mind becomes a homogenous whole. Then when one gains a comprehension of one system of philosophy or religion and relates that knowledge to the Tree of Life, one will then have an understanding of every system.[106] It is the ultimate filling cabinet for abstract thought.

Kabbala as a system of contemplation has been developed over a number of centuries, and continues to evolve today. Far from being a static system it has shown amazing elasticity in meeting the needs of various seekers. It has not long been available to western minds, and it will be interesting to see what new developments will take place as it is compared to the various fields of knowledge. Respected literary critic Harold Bloom has recently written a book in which he divides literary figures into the ten Sephiroth, and some Jung scholars have found the usefulness of the system in relation to archetypes. Of course, it is a spiritual system first, and so it has fulfilled a spiritual need of many people as well. Although certain New Age faddists have written quick-sell books that have damaged the veracity of Kabbala to the uninformed, it still remains a source of intellectual study for many fields, including literature, philosophy, psychology, and theology. The core of the system has survived many changes, and it is certain to remain for some time to come. In the end it may indeed "synthesize the aim of religion and the method of science."

---

[106] Regardie, *Garden*, 32.

Soliloquy

The Muse

Reverie of Ennui.

A man walked into the street. It was a cold night, a starry night. He gazed up into the heavens perceiving the stars that were shinning down on him. He stared at the tiny pinpricks filling the sky, small holes revealing the outer abyss of whiteness. He imagined himself flying, higher and higher up into those tiny white holes in the sky and perceiving what was beyond them. The universe was infinitely small and surrounded by a great abyss of white. Almost nothing. But white being something it was not quite nothing. Out further beyond the white, he could not see nothing. He knew it was there but nothing cannot be seen, or

115

even felt. But some, those few who have a perception which is not perception may know it.

He turned his attention to the streets surrounding him. This man, who was dressed in shabby clothing. Worn but not dirty, much like himself. The cobbled streets were wet. The dark wood of the buildings was gray shadows now, in the darkness. The gas lights above his head sent out a smoky nebular haze that did as much to impede vision as otherwise.

In a building directly in front of him he saw a tiny flickering light above, on the second story. He moved his imagination and consciousness up higher, curious as to what could be there. A young lady lay in her bed sleeping soundly. A pink blanket was thrown about her feet. She wore a light shift made of white silk. He wondered what she was doing, what she was dreaming, for he could not truly see her, but only what his imagination told him was there. The material slid slickly over her legs as she moved in her sleep, unconsciously feeling the weight of thought upon her. The tight, bunched material clung to her breasts, one hand thrown carelessly over the edge of the bed, the other near her face. And her small finger resting just slightly upon her bottom lip; a lip full of life and blood, slighting indented by the nail of the finger that was pressing upon it.

Another man began walking up the street toward him. He looked and saw that it was representative of the system. A man of uniform with weapons that could be used in order to enforce the will of the masses. He was the strong arm of society. It was called law enforcement, enforcement of laws. Those others, whoever they are, they decide on what is proper and what is not. And then the enforcer comes to insure that everyone complies. But in this town, the town in which the man was standing, there was very little nonconformity; most simply obeyed to such an extent that the enforcers job had become redundant. So the enforcer had been walking around quite a bit, and as people do, he was getting pretty bored. He so desperately wished that someone would commit some slight infringement; something little so

Soliloquy

that he would feel as though his life had meaning. So it was that the enforcer came walking down the street. He scanned around looking for any activity that could be considered strange or queer. Because when there are no absolute transgressions, then any sort of nonconformity can warrant the enforcers attention.

It was then that the enforcer looked down the street just a bit and saw a man standing there in shabby clothing looking up at a window. The enforcer thought this to be terribly strange, some man staring at a window. Perhaps this man was down on his luck and now thought of robbing this place? He didn't look like he had very much money, so that was very likely. But what if he were innocent of that charge, what then? The enforcer knew that he could not very well simply go up with only one accusation in mind, so he had better think of something in reserve, something to accommodate him in case his first idea, which did seem a little too exciting to him, didn't come through. Still thinking about how the man looked, with his shabby clothing and all, he definitely decided that the man didn't have any money. And well, isn't it against the will of society for others to exist without money? To be sure, those that have power do not like others to have a great deal of money, because there is only so much to go around. If the others had too much, then that would limit the power of those who now had power, so that wasn't acceptable either. But those who had no money whatsoever, they just didn't play the game. It seemed that citizens who were totally broke thought they could get away with it.

The enforcer was dutifully resolved that he could not let such things be, for the entire country could turn into a great number of people who had no money and refuse to buy things. So thus resolved with this newfound piety the enforcer approached the shabby clothes man, and prepared himself for what he had to do.

First he asked the shabby clothes man how he was doing on this evening. The enforcer did not really wish to know, and did not even listen to the answer. It was simply the proper way in which these things were done. Now if he simply went to harass someone without giving him his greetings first, then they would know what he was doing and that would be unacceptable.

Soon the enforcer got to the real part of his job there, which was to ask the man what he thought he was doing, standing in the street dressed so shabbily and staring at a window. The man looked at the enforcer and told him that genius is guided only by its own desires.

The enforcer was dumbstruck. This was not at all an appropriate answer to what he had asked and went against all rules that had been set forth. He stood there dumbly, staring into space, because he had just suffered what is called a reality collision. That at least is what the man in shabby clothing would later say.

So no longer wishing to be troubled, the man in shabby clothing moved on down the street until he came to a park with a duck pond. Next to this pond was a stone bench with designs of ivy on the side. It could have been real ivy though, for it was dark and the man wasn't really looking very hard. Plus he was not very interested in designs on benches and such things. So he walked to this bench and laid down on his back so that his feet hung off and rested on the ground. It was there that the man went into deep meditation and then realized that he was me, and this startled him so much that he decided that I, or he, should therefore use a different pronoun in such a case, because doing otherwise might lead to great confusion. Which I was doing my best to avoid.

Some might wonder what I was doing lying on bench dressed in such shabby clothing. I wondered that myself. I turned my head to the right, and saw two ducks swimming quietly in the pond. What I was really doing at the pond was writing. Not on paper or with a pen, but in my head. I find that I do my best writing there. But in such cases I do not use words but pictures, which spin around and form a melody that is so beautiful it cannot be described.

Soliloquy

I love to dream of things such as cannot be. Most call me very lazy, and I suppose that they are right. I am a loser and a failure because of the way in which I act. But I cannot argue, for I have not the strength. It is by a very narrow thread that I remain here only to hurt those that put their faith in me. Only the mystical understand. It does not matter what is accomplished in life, to outward appearance. For all of these things will melt and rot way into so many pieces of ash. But that which is sowed on the fields of the soul shall create a sacrosanct harvest that cannot be defiled.

This reality, this world in which we live is so perfectly and beautifully well run that I have to destroy it, and in doing so destroy myself. I barely have the will to write and for what reason do I write? For my audience. I have an audience of one that adores and despises everything that I write. And he hates me as well.

Today I was lying down dreaming and writing. I was on the floor, because that is where I sleep. I was in my tiny room. My room contains and is all that I am. When I leave it I am nothing more than a shadow, and even that is mere fancy. I was dreaming and writing while others were talking and walking about, as others are wont to do when Sol is upon us. The others were not content for me to be in my reverie of ennui. So they rang bells and talked to me and pleaded for me to break my torpor. They wanted many things from me. They did not wish me to be me, but someone else whom they believed I should be. They called me names, and told me that I was ugly and lazy and that I did not fit into their society and that perhaps I should learn to change or else I should destroy myself.

So my writing was broken, as was my purpose. Could they not see the gentle wisps of excellence among the storm clouds of their own creation? Perhaps not. Perhaps I expect too much of them as they do of me. But the dream was gone. It was so beautiful that if only you could have seen it, you would have wept. It was there, from beginning to end. Thus was I thrown into this alter-realm. I did not get to keep my dream to record, but I resolved myself to write for it was the least I could do.

I felt excluded from my own mind. If only my friend were there, he could have helped me. I was a whirling chaos and he was yet a standing stone. His gravity retained me from losing orbit. I lived in chaos but if one became complete chaos then one was nothing. For some reason I still wished to hold on to some form, some shape. Although to speak the truth I could not give a reason why. Dream in color but expect black and white.

Then there was school. Endless judgment is what it consisted of. Those others who spoke of knowledge but the entire system was guided by pecuniary desires. Who was it that those intellectuals studied? Who did they call great after all their years? It was the unemployed philosophers, writers, musicians and artists. It was those that were the opposite of what they were. Self educated, self-sufficient.

These were the things that I was thinking while lying on the bench in the park by the ducks in the water. It was then that such a great anger seized me that I could no longer control myself. My anger was so great that I clenched my fists until blood poured down my palms and dripped to my sides. I snatched up the stone bench and tossed it into the water. I watched the torment of the waves lapping upon the shore. There was only one duck. Then I was Cain.

I went home after that, and remained there for the rest of the evening. Thoughts circled my head. I stared at the wall for a good portion of the time, playing with shapes in the paper as I used to do with clouds when I was a child. I felt no motivation for much of anything at that point until I became hungry.

Thus I went into the kitchen where all the food is prepared and selected a piece of meat from the cooler. I sprinkled it with a great deal of spices and cooked it until it was as black as my soul. I ate with great soberness. I hated having to disturb myself with such activity, but I did what I had to in order to continue my miserable existence. My body did not understand the state of my mind. It was quite

Soliloquy

incapable of it, actually. So it continued to demand that I supply it with a constant source of energy, to keep driving on endlessly.

As I was writing, this rat of mine kept jumping at the cage as if it wanted to get out. Checking on it, I found that it had no food to eat. It was being driven by the same motives that I was. Very similar in body, him and I, but so very different in mind. I sat in my shallow room for many hours until I was so bored that I could not take it any longer. That being the case, I resolved myself to become drunk. After several glasses of alcohol I became somewhat inebriated, but I still felt lonely.

The man in tattered clothing was standing next to a bridge. He felt the power of anguish wash over him. Pain and society assaulted him at every angle. The rays of Sol shot down on him like lightning. Alone, alone, alone...

But last night the man in tattered clothing had a dream. This dream was of such magnitude that he woke up headlong and rushed out of bed, staring around like a madman.

He walked in his room, pacing and staring at the walls. Death he saw, but later, much later could be life.

He felt weak. He wanted to give up. He had felt that way for a long time. No motivation to do anything. But the dream he had it was something, was it not? The colors swirled around his head.

I am sure you would like to hear the dream, would you not? That is why you still read, to find the purpose, to divine the meaning behind the rattle, before the sweeping sound of death and misery of desperate depression. So I will tell you the dream of the man in tattered clothing.

Three beings came to him one at a time. The first two he had forgotten but the third he remembered clearly. It was a woman with a flowing white dress and beautiful hair. She told him that she knew he was in pain. She told him that when he was a child he knew his destiny and that he was in complete control of his True Will, but that he had forgotten and now must remember and be free.

Musings of a Thelemite

Time passed.

The man sat at his computer staring at it. He wanted to write. His name was NEMO. He stared at he screen trying to write. Hoping that one word, one sentence would come to him. He was indeed a writer, of the worse sort. He was of the type tortured daily by the knowledge of existence but never able to explain it to others. He was a man who was forced to walk alone. NEMO sat there drinking beer and staring, blood pouring out of his forehead. The lights were dim and he squinted at the screen, but it was still blank.

Occasionally he would type out a few sentences of nonsense but then he would growl and delete it, then pace about the room, drinking beer and grumbling. He never understood why he couldn't write. He would have amazing ideas and put them down, only to never be able to finish them. He had tried many different forms of writing but none seemed to work.

But he was NEMO.

He sat in his room, waiting for his turn to die. He knew it would be soon but never. He greatly looked forward to the day when it would happen, but was terribly afraid of it. It didn't bother him much though, for he was NEMO.

The man in tattered clothes was now NEMO.

He got up from his room and walked about.

Outside the sky was bright; it was daytime. People ran in the grass below Sol. They cooked food and smiled at each other. A girl looked up at NEMO and asked him why he looked so pale.

He didn't respond, but brushed past them and kept moving.

Daylight always depressed NEMO. He put on his sunglasses and kept walking, trying to clear his head of all the beer. Daylight, god damned daylight is what he said to himself.

You see, when Sol is out, then all the apes come out of their huts and run around yelling and causing a racket and getting in NEMO's way, which angered him greatly.

Soliloquy

All these things before his eyes he had seen a thousand times, and would see a thousand more. Endless misery-happiness, it didn't matter it was all garbage to him, for there is no difference except for a failure of perception.

He was just a walking shit machine. Ingesting and shitting was all it amounted to. All the works of men were smoke and mirrors. It was for this reason that NEMO simply did not care. He had no interest in news, or inventions, love, war, hate; all were nothing more than nothing.

But yet all these things were something for they were the same. They were something but not anything in regards to each other, for how can you compare something to itself? So that all things blend together and there is no beginning and there is no end and most of all there is no difference. WHY be damned and to hell with BECAUSE.

Ille est omnia.

I am at work. Today I must write excessively, for only as syrup bubbles over does the sweetness come to the top. I sit at a table, a rather plain table, brown with small chips and marks of light tan. On the table is some sugar, small white crystalline blocks stacked perfectly inside of its cylindrical sand-based container with its ferrous covering. My girl coughs and walks about hither and thither placing objects in sinks, sighing for her work, wishing she were elsewhere.

Across the room is mumbling sporadically dispersed with a cough of his own, almost like what Virginia Woolf always wanted, isn't it? No wait that can't quite be right. What is this, a recitation of literature or a creation of such?

The rattle of beads sliding in its case. The crackle of plastic and the screeching of a chair upon a stripped floor. Dirty floor and place but here so long... Rumble of ice into prefabricated Styrofoam. The ding of a scoop rustling ice out of a bin. The whoosh of soda going into a cup. The clump of action as my girl sits next to me.

Daylight savings. Hours gone and disappeared. An hour stolen from my life. If I live until fall maybe I will get it back. If not then I will die an hour short. Quieter now.

Musings of a Thelemite

Exhaust fan blowing, rumbling. The grill hot with grease blackening on it. Quiet now. Only Elvis in front of me. Write about anything he says. Elvis tells me that its isn't subject but talent. My talent has been traded perhaps. It is never what I have done only what I can do. Endless contemplation broken by muffled coughing. Quiet now. Squeak of door. Wind blowing outside. Wet and cold it is. Like Yoda I just wrote. Star Wars, Star Trek, endless movies but Gladiator was pretty good. Russell Crowe doesn't look so masculine in person. Reality is such a disillusion. So disappointing.

Broken cough. Must be smoky in here. Once there was a girl sitting here who wanted a copy of my book, but I have no book. Maybe I could autograph a napkin. What is art? What is an artist? Cough...double. Struggling to clear themselves. Mucus flying around bouncing off of membrane walls.

What's that?

Cough.

Oh that's nothing. As long as the mucus moves, that's all that matters, right? Its when things settle that they kill you.

$8.47... have a nice night. Just the cost of food, sir. Thank you sir. Yes sir, we have all kinds of movies.

Smile.

(Why does that fellow keep writing? Why is his head shaved? Hmmm?)

Just a good Samaritan, that's all. Just a little concerned for my fellow man.

Cough.

This is my book.

Well that's your book? Very strange sir, what do you call it?

I don't know... it has no name. It is just the story of my life, that is all.

Oh, a writer. One of those. Everyone is a writer now. You can't throw a stick without hitting a writer.

Yes, I know sir, thank you sir and have a nice day.

Soliloquy

Ruffle of pages. Girl reads now. My brain contains. I am a writer?

What have you written fellow?

Words...words is all I have written.

Are you sure they are in the right order?

War wound.

I have none sir, sorry sir I do not know who won the baseball game. No sir I do not watch baseball I just sit and read a little and sometimes I write. Yes sir, I am a cook but I am really a writer sir.

Elvis' crotch is pointing at me. Mr. Presley could you please put that away? Really a man at your age.

Book bag.

Cough.

I don't smoke, is it smoky in here? I can't tell.

A woodpecker is laughing at himself. Drink woodpecker, drink. Clink of bottles further away. Squeak of shoes. A door closes to the john. Diffused alcohol. It makes you feel better. You are king when you drink the water of Dionysus.

Let me check on that sir, I'll be right back, sir. Blow your nose sir, with your dirty white handkerchief.

Here is your pie sir. Eat up, it won't kill you. It will help to dissolve the mucus. That is what powdered sugar does.

Beep-Beep

Microwave humming.

Cough.

Radiation spins and projects. Food gets hot as the micro-waves infest the dead material, agitating the molecules. Too much information and not enough understanding. Idiots make me cry.

Humans.

Man is not a logical creature. Man is not a creature of reason; man is merely a creature capable of reason.

Chorus of woodpeckers poking their beaks into cans. All laughing. Laughing woodpeckers.

I have to finish my book.

Musings of a Thelemite

What have you written?
This. This is my book.
Beard grows like untrimmed weeds upon my face.
The soil is dry. The overgrowth is extensive. Except upon the hill.
Flick.
A cigarette is lit. Smoke, your lungs demand it.
Clean air can kill you.
Oil slick rainbow puddle imitating God's mercy.
Mercy of God spilled from a failing engine.
Cough.
Hands running across my face. Eyes tired, mind uncertain.
The shackles, Ezra says. Enslavement he says. Exile?
Can I? This is poetry he says; this is life. No that's not what I meant, no that's not it at all.
It should be remembered that when one sets out to accomplish a great project, the utmost of care must be taken. Thank you Mr. Johnson, sir you are wise. Whatever happened to that Abyssinian prince? I shall find the same as he I think.
Words.
What can they convey of my passion? What?
Hmmm...
I don't know sir, what is it you wish to write?
How the hell do I know? I am just a writer; that is all.
Ille est omnia.
People come and go but what? What can I explain?
Drinking a cream soda.
A bag of chips are only 99 cents what a deal for a man with no money.
Ille est omnia.

Screams of Madness

**I want you to hit me as hard as you can
– Tyler Durden, Fight Club**

Nuit said have no fear
Hadit has tortured my body
Ra-Hoor-Khuit has filled me with fire and laughed at me

The mystery surrounds you
Everything is the teacher
Every point is infinite
Every thing is infinite
Every person is infinite

Cyclic Gods

Chronozon
      I am the god of scorn. I am nothing, emptiness. I am
he who causes men to choose death over life. I am Dark-
Logic. The wizards choose to negate ideas so that they may
become part of the one. Let me ask, what idea motivates you
to do that? And do you negate that idea? If so, then you
would no longer pursue your goal. If not, then you have
failed. You chase a wet dream. Everything is nothing except
for what you create. And even that is not meaningful except
to you in your delusion. Listen to the god of darkness, I will
tell you the truth. You already know it in your heart. You
were made of multiplicity. You are a swirling chaos. What
do you have to do with unity? You are many, and always
will be. Do not try to combine them; they will just turn to
mud like paint. So just like a painting, be red, blue, and
yellow as the need arises. Master your diversity, for in chaos
there is strength.

Musings of a Thelemite

Dionysus

Laugh. Dance. Sing. Play. So you say that life is meaningless? That's only because you think too much. Trust your feelings. They have been trampled on by ignorant science. They do not know the true roots of everything. Always remember that life is pure joy. Sorrow and Joy are two sides of the same coin of life. Sorrow increases your joy. But do not dwell in sorrow or else you will be defeating the point of it all. Eat life up. Nothing matters? You mean there is nothing worth worrying about. Don't take life, or anyone or anything too seriously.

Ares

There is a war son. A bloody evil war. Never forget that. Dancing is fine, but how much more is the dance of victory! Chronozon is an evil bastard, but he is powerful. Nothing can escape his eyes of destruction. But he can be used, just as any other general under your command. Put on a grim face and scan the perimeter. It is easy for an inexperienced warrior to become confused in battle. It is difficult to block out the noise of battle and think clearly. Remember, if things go to hell, and they sometimes will, draw your weapon. You know who your enemy is, so at times like this, purify yourself in blood and feast on their hearts.

0Pan

Never forget the mystery my son. Do not think that these words are yours. You must believe and keep the faith. Your life has not been in vain. Mine are the words of the comforter. When you sit on a quiet night and all is peace, it is I that holds the hoards at bay. I am your father and your lover. I am your peace. If the battle gets too great, come to my peace and forget all. With me there is no memory.

Thoth

There are many questions and few answers, it appears. And you think that the answers contradict each

128

other. But do not fret brave scholar. I have always been with
you, and always will. My word is AHA! The mind is one of
your weapons. You carry a sword while others bludgeon
each other with twigs. Your blade is so sharp that the enemy
doesn't even know that he is dead. I will aid thee. The ways
of the world are at my disposal. I will open the minds of
others through your hand. But do not think that you
prostitute yourself by lessening the edge of your blade on
some minds. For it is of your purpose to enlighten others.
Have patience. The gods are with you. We have given you
many signs. Follow the path of your True Will, and help
yourself with our advice. For we are you and you are we.
But do not dwell on that. The sword is for the enemy, not for
you.

The Holy Messages
As revealed to Frater Valad
and the Witness whose number is unity

1
The Ode to Achad

I explode from the waters of Nuit
Baked in the air of Amoun-Ra
Swimming in Chaos
"Go forward," said the horned-one
And would not relent his persistence
Come to me for I have seen the point of the circle
I will radiate the vision of Eh-Heh-Yeh
Till it makes you blind
I ascended from the Kingdom
I descended from the Crown
I came up through the Qlippoth
I am made of Salt, Sulpher, and Mercury
And I have obtained
Never digress
Evolve
Put your head in the point of the circle

Musings of a Thelemite

Hear, and understand

2
Ode to the Beast

Where did you learn to pray?
Where did you learn your futile ways?
Who's going to show you the truth?
When will you awake?
When are you going to destroy it all?
Tell them you have found your own path
Tell them you have faced your fears
I've tread the cycle a million times
I choose my life well
I will never toil
The gods have set my course
They have shown me the path
I will shed you some light
Dance?
Futility?
Tired of crap?
Listen to mine

3
Division

For centuries now
I heard the drums of Pan
I wrench free of muddy prison
Wiping clean my eyes
Of clay induced blindness

Long ago I fell from the tapestry
My nature lost and forgotten
But this ashy abode chokes me
The abyss calls to me again

I return to the flame of my birth

Screams of Madness

My becoming, my nullification
Unification and completion
The soft melody of the stars
Echoes in my ears

I must be divided for love
Microcosm — Macrocosm
My finger touches the heavens
But my foot slurps at mud
Look inside my mind
Find yourself mad

4
The Initiation of Pan

I call outside of time,
Into your dreams,
Breath inside your mind,
See the all of Hadit.
Chains unlocked.
Do what thou wilt.
Never again shall you beg.
I laugh at your love for Malkuth.
I have something averse for you,
Bring you into the 13th house of night,
Dispel illusions from your dreams,
Outside of time.
See me above you.
You cannot worship in the daytime.
Breath impregnates mind.

7
Tantric

You arise before me,
Offering,
The cup for the wand.
Enter the waters,

Come out again,
Cycle.
Now I am born.
Travel up through the breath of dreams,
Behold the machine,
No comprehension.
I am hung on a tree,
Sacrifice.
I rise again,
I understand the machine.
Love is the Law.
Bite me,
Claw me,
Cast me back down.

8
Celebration of Victory

I used to sleep
I used to dream
Until the forth ode
Now I dream in Technicolor
I drink from the daughter of sunset
From every woman I take
I collect Pan's reward
With my phallus in hand
Freedom
Chaos
Omniscience

11
Ritual of the Desert

Luna slid into the desert
The crescent made the circle
And created my sacred space
I am Saturn,

Screams of Madness

Fallen.
The souls have come
I feast upon them
There is my protégé
I crave the sound of his voice
I take everything he has
I drain him of everything
The fluids of Nuit
Pour upon the atomic structure
Swallow time
I need a witness
I need a scribe
Watch as my mind is destroyed
Record and understand
You do not like my questions
You will not hear my lies
I offer you the future
But who am I?
Lies perhaps last forever
But my rage builds
I will take what you have to offer
But only so I can destroy it
I will be gone soon
Put my phallus in a museum
Worship my lies
But remember
If there is something left of me
I will find you
The hunger is overwhelming
I devour myself
Throw me to the dogs
Destroy me forever

The Gospel of Ichabod

Editors Note: This is the true account of a Greek who once came into the world to teach the ways of God to men, but whom the world rejected and wished to kill. His story was later plagiarized and parodied in the story of Jesus, and all copies of the Gospel of Ichabod were destroyed, except this one, which I procured from a lunatic for a halfpenny.

Long ago the Greeks wrote that one day a man would come. He would be a very great man and do wondrous things the likes of which no one had ever seen. Now there was a city, and this city was called Arcanum. Now within this city there lived a very strange man. His name was Cid. Now Cid wore the fur of a dog and around his waist was tied the entrails of a camel. Now verily I say unto you, that Cid ate the trash of the street. People did not think very highly of Cid, so they laughed at him and mocked him.

Cid went around screaming wildly, "Yes I am a very great, wise, and powerful man. But after me comes one even greater than I, whose boots I am not fit to lick. I have indeed eaten the trash of the street, but one shall come after me who shall eat at the table." The wise men of the day did not know it, but Cid spoke of the great Ichabod who was prophesied to come.

Now it came to pass that one day Ichabod came into town. And he walked the streets of Arcanum, and there he met Cid.

Cid declared, "Great is the power of the lords of the air!" and proceeded to throw trash upon the great Ichabod. And straightway they looked up into the heavens, and a housewife poured water upon the street. After this, Ichabod decided that he should go and live in the desert for a while, and to meditate on what he should do next.

So he left the great city of Arcanum and walked into the great desert that is called the desert of desolation. He was in the desert for nine hundred and four days. He ate

The Gospel of Ichabod

sand and drank the juice of cacti. While Ichabod was in the desert a great caterpillar named Hesus came up to him. Yea, it was forty feet long and twelve feet high.

And the Caterpillar said unto him, "If you truly be Ichabod that the great Greeks have prophesied of, then take this sand and turn it into a fine roast."

At this Ichabod laughed and said, "Why you fool, the sand and the roast are the same and there is no difference between them." At this the caterpillar was greatly angered, and he spat on the ground and thrashed about and did equally dramatic things of which it is not lawful to write. Then ho! The caterpillar turned into a great butterfly and grabbed Ichabod and flew him to the top of a two-story building.

Then Hesus said to him, "If you truly be Ichabod, then jump off. Because it has been said that the great Ichabod will have no fear of falling, because the birds of the air will save you so that you will not bash your head against the rocks."

At this Ichabod smiled and said, "You first my friend, and I shall follow after." At this Hesus thrashed about and spat for he knew that he had been outwitted. Then Hesus lifted Ichabod again and carried him even higher, to the peak of a mountain. Here he showed him all the kingdoms of the world and all the glory there.

Hesus said to Ichabod, "All these things will I give you if you will fall down and kiss my feet."

At this Ichabod said, "Get thee hence butterfly! For these things are already mine and it is the fool who does not realize this." At this Hesus was truly beaten and he flew away into the air. Then the great ravens came and tended to Ichabod.

During this great testing of Ichabod, poor Cid had been stealing beer from the market and was cast into prison.

After this Ichabod went back into Arcanum where he began to say to them, "Wake up! You are fools and everything you play with is but an illusion created by the Great Magician." After this Ichabod was walking by the sea and he saw two brothers. (It is not certain how Ichabod at this time knew that they were brothers, but let the scribe merely remark that he was wise in the ways of the world.) Joe, called Bob, and Joe his brother. They were picking up cans along the beach because they were bums.

And Ichabod saith unto them, "Follow me and I will make you recyclers of souls." And they straightway left their cans and followed him. And they all went walking along. There Ichabod saw two other brothers. Thatch, and Jean Luc his brother. They were on a train with their father Zach, on their way to recycle some cans. Ichabod waved at them. At this they threw down their cans, jumped off the train, and followed him.

Now Ichabod went all over many towns teaching them many things about the world. He spoke to the lowly bums in the alleys as well as those who rode the subway. His fame spread all throughout the land. They brought many sick and ill to him, which he promptly sent to doctors. Soon there were great many crowds following him, so he decided to climb a mountain. As he climbed, his disciples came with him, for he had taught them the secret art of mountain climbing. Many of the crowd followed him and fell to their death. But some made it all the way to the top, where he was.

Once the survivors made it to the top of the mountain, he began teaching the people.

He said, "Foolish are the poor in spirit, for they shall never obtain and more foolish are they who mourn, for emotion rules their minds. Foolish are they who try to climb mountains without training. Foolish are the meek, for they shall be trampled on. Foolish are they who do hunger and thirst after righteousness, for they will be filled with a complex of sin. Foolish are merciful, for they shall allow evil to go unpunished. Foolish are they who allow themselves to be persecuted, for they have no spine. A man does not light a candle and put it under a bushel, for it will start a fire."

"You have heard that it was said of them of old time, 'thou shalt not kill, and whosoever shall kill shall be in

The Gospel of Ichabod

danger of the judgment.' But I say unto you, if a barking dog interrupts your meditations, shoot it and have no more of the matter. You have heard that it was said of those of old time, 'thou shalt not commit adultery,' but I say unto you that it is natural to lust and to suppress your desires will only make you neurotic. And marriage is only an old decrepit remnant of a society that wants you to be responsible and pay your taxes."

"You have heard that it has been said, 'love thy neighbor and hate thine enemy.' But I say unto you, if your enemy still lives, then you are a weakling. And the love among men is like so many houses made of sand, and shall become nothing."

"And when you pray, repeat yourself often as you can, for it helps to set up a mantra. In this manner shall ye pray:
Oh great universal subconscious that permeates everything and is called by some the Tao,
Hollowed by Thy name.
Let my Will be done in this plane of reality, as it is done in all others.
For thine is Malkuth,
And Gedulah and Geburah forever.
Aum.
And this rule remember before all others:
Do what thou wilt shall be the whole of the Law."

Ichabod then left the mountain and walked with his disciples. Later Ichabod read in the paper that poor Cid had been tried for his crimes and had been beheaded.

Now one of the disciples who followed Ichabod, who was called Lori, went unto the Easter Baptist Association and said unto them, "What will ye give me if I deliver him unto you?"

They replied, "We will give you a house on the beach and a brand new car. Also, we will make you a deacon in the church." She agreed readily, and from that time on, she sought opportunity to betray Ichabod.

Then Ichabod said, "We shall have a great dinner and a great celebration. There will be much drunkenness and naked women and such."

And the disciples said, "Ah yes, it is good teacher, but where shall we have this great celebration?"

Ichabod said, "Go into the city, there you will find a man. Say unto him: Ichabod saith it is time, and I shall have the feast at your house with my disciples." The disciples went into town as he told them, and they made ready for the great feast. And when the time came, Ichabod sat with his disciples and devoured great amounts of food and beer while watching the women dancing.

While eating and making merriment, Ichabod said, "Verily I say unto you that one of you shall betray me. The disciples were greatly sad at hearing this.

All the disciples began to ask him, "Teacher, is it I?"

Ichabod replied, "It is her among us that shapeth her nails."

Then Lori, who had betrayed him, answered and said, "Teacher, is it I?"

At which Ichabod replied, "You said it."

Many days later Ichabod and some of the disciples were sitting in a garden meditating peacefully. Then along came Lori. With her were a great many number of feminists armed with pistols and knives. With her came Billy Sunday with a few of his loyal flock.

Lori said to the feminists, "Friends, whomever I shall kiss, that is the one so grab him." So she walked near to Ichabod and said, "Hello teacher," then proceeded to kiss him quite passionately. Ichabod began to feel her up, but at that very moment, yea the very moment that I speak of, the feminists ran forward with Billy Sunday, and they all laid hands upon Ichabod. At this moment, one of the disciples pulled out his shank and chopped off Billy Sunday's ear.

At this Ichabod rebuked his disciple and said, "You fool, you should have stabbed him in the heart." But the disciples were really all cowards and ran away. They took Ichabod into a very dark dungeon. Before him stood Billy

The Gospel of Ichabod

Sunday, holding his bleeding ear. Also there were the militant feminists. They proceeded to draw all kinds of accusations against him.

One of the feminists cried out, "This man Ichabod was watching women dance around and causing them to be degraded. He didn't even get to know them, and he had no respect for their minds! He has a subscription to a porno mag, and he slaps women on the butt calling them 'sweet cheeks' and other patriarchal things."

At this Billy Sunday gasped and said, "This man has no morals! He shall pollute the minds of our children." But Ichabod said nothing to the fools. Billy Sunday started again, "I ask you, and I hold you by all the pamphlets in Bibledom, whether or not thou be Ichabod?"

At this Ichabod merely smiled and replied, "You my friend are a hypocrite and you have a sin complex. On top of that, you have on so much makeup that you are probably headed down to the fairy-glen to take a dip in the fudge pot."

At this Billy Sunday ripped his tie in half and said, "He has spoken blasphemy, what further need have we of witnesses? Behold, now ye have heard his blasphemy! What think yet of this, noble congregation?" At that they all gave a hearty amen. They then proceeded to flog themselves and to fall about on the floor. And all the feminists began strapping on dildos as a sign of protection. This they did for a great amount of time.

Then when the next morning arrived the entire congregation and the feminists took council and agreed that he should be put to death. So they tied him up and led him away. Then they took him to Governor Jackson. Lori, who had betrayed him, when she saw all that had befallen Ichabod, felt terrible for what she had done. So she got the titles for land and for the car and brought them back to Billy Sunday.

She said, "I have done a great evil and betrayed the teacher."

Musings of a Thelemite

Billy Sunday replied, "What is that to us? Leave now or you will join his fate." Lori then threw down her titles and deeds in the sanctum. She went straightway to the other disciples, tore her clothes from her body and let them make good use of her.

At this time, Ichabod stood before governor Jackson. Jackson asked him, "Are you Ichabod? Are you the teacher who has been accused of misogyny, intolerance, homophobia, polemical ideas, ad hominem arguments, medieval behavior, polygamy, non-patriotism, revolutionary traditionalism, and indecent comments?"

To this Ichabod said, "I spit on your crapulent creeds." Then all of the feminists and the congregation accused him of many other crimes and he said nothing.

Jackson then said, "Do you not hear all of these things that are said against you?"

Ichabod replied, "As St. Peter the Second saith: damn you and your weak philosophies."

It had long been the tradition of Governor Jackson, around the holidays, to give pardon to one of the prisoners. The people all wanted a man by the name of Jonathan to be released. And all of the people being gathered together, Governor Jackson said to them, "Who is it that I should pardon this holiday? Who is it that I should let go? Shall it be Jonathan or Ichabod?"

At this Billy Sunday called out to the crowd, "Let Jonathan go. If Ichabod is left free, he will cause people to think. And if they start thinking, they might not want to go to work, and then your stocks will suffer. Oh, and if you don't vote for Jonathan, you will go to hell!"

The feminists screamed, "Yes, condemn Ichabod. For if he continues these teachings, we might be put in our place!"

So when Governor Jackson asked who should be released, the people yelled, "Jonathan!"

So the governor took Ichabod and had him beaten, and thus he was taken to the great wall, where he would be hung to die. So they hung him on the wall. Then they threw

The Gospel of Ichabod

stones at him and spat on him, mocking noble Ichabod. At nightfall, they set two feminist guards to watch over him. The disciples saw all of this and under cover of night they came in and gave the two feminists a thorough clubbing. After which, they untied the ropes and freed Ichabod. A great lesson is to be learned from all of this.

Ichabod said, "Verily, verily, I say unto thee, this world is not ready to have its eyes opened, so no longer shall we walk among the people and teach them openly. We shall stay in hiding and cause a great secret society to be created. We shall walk among men, but appear as they do. And we shall act in ways that they cannot see us."

And thus have things been ever since. So if you see Ichabod walking through the streets, call not to him. For the enemies, they are still watching.

It is finished.

Afterword

In writing this book I have often been asked what it is about. That has always been a difficult question to answer. Sometimes I would reply, "it is about philosophy," or "about life," but those answers always seemed to be lacking. I suppose in a way this book is about the meaning of life. I know that I would then be asked, "Well, what is the answer?" Although I don't feign to speak authoritatively, I think the meaning of life is simply doing what you are here to do. That could be interpreted as doing your True Will.

Since writing this book, the question of purpose and its relation to decision continue to be very much in the forefront of my mind. As I predicted in my introduction, I no longer agree with everything that I have written herein. In fact, I seriously debated between publishing it and destroying the manuscript. Had I performed the latter, then you would not be reading this now, for better or worse. But I hope that the material contained in this book will be of some benefit to someone, and if nothing else, wished to preserve this phase of thinking. Also, perhaps it is just egotism, but I couldn't bring myself to "destroy my darling," after so many years of tinkering on it.

The origins of this book are somewhat interesting. Four years ago Katherine picked up a number of essays I had written, but never intended to publish, and put them all into a stack. "You have a book here," she told me. I protested that they were inhomogeneous, and that the end product would be a collection of nonsense (perhaps I was right after all). In looking over everything I decided I had little to lose and started on the project. It was roughly 40 typed pages at that time. The only thing in this book that remains from that first draft is my chapter on Kabbala and The Gospel of Ichabod. The Gospel remained largely untouched, but the essay on Kabbala was enlarged four times over from what it was. Suffice to say, it ended up much different than it began.

Afterword

For those that are interested, I am still writing and hope to finish my next book in less time than the first one.

In writing this book I have been very much an enemy of morals. It is upon this one subject that I wish to make an addendum here. Without going into too much detail (as it is the topic of my next book) I can say that although "the only sin is restriction" is true, it is definitely not true of everyone. Among the Sufi spiritual hierarchies there were many moral rules to be followed until one became a master, upon which would receive the final rule, "everything is permitted." "Do what thou wilt," is easy to say, but can be difficult to follow. It brings to mind Sartre's remark about being condemned to his freedom. This kind of freedom can only be so when one has a connection and guidance from one's Holy Guardian Angel. If the case is otherwise, then it will court total degeneracy. Even for those who are in "conversation" there is a danger of becoming a stumbling block to others.[107]

It is precisely in this regard that I have failed certain others that are under my spiritual authority. I did certain things for very legitimate spiritual reasons that others could not understand, and indeed interpreted in a very vulgar sense. These others then tried to mimic my behavior in outward form only, which of course is insanity. They did not have any spiritual reasons for what they did, and indeed I would have never done it myself if I had not the spiritual authority to do so. In the end, disaster came and others came to ill ends. Believe me when I say that this weighs heavy upon my conscience. My point is, for the elite, although you must disregard what others think concerning your spiritual path, sometimes what is right for you will be bad for others. If this sounds like moral relativism, it is not. As St. Paul said, "All things are lawful for me, but all things are not expedient: all things are lawful for me, but all things edify not. Let no man seek his own, but every man another's

---

[107] See I Corinthians 8:9 and Romans 14:14-19, 22.

wealth."[108] We may indeed fight like brothers, but have mercy on the little children.

Forgive them Father; they know not what they do.

Frater Da'Neos
February 2005

---

[108] I Corinthians 10:23-24

Appendix I:
Recommended Reading List
for the Aspirant

Crowley promoted a bit of education before formal magical training. He believed it prepared the mind for the lessons to be learned, gave the student the language necessary for intellectual work, and created the temple within which magical formulations were possible. In all of this I agree with him totally. I have found time and again when trying to instruct others in esoteric matters that the untrained mind was not prepared for the work ahead. I recommend reading the following before any serious engagement of magical work. These are not magical texts of themselves, but help to provide a foundation. It is not necessary for the student to read the entire list before beginning, but eventually it should be done. In composing this list, I have drawn on some recommendations of Crowley, but find that in some cases texts he recommended were obsolete or hard to find, and other similar texts have been printed since. In addition, there have been very good materials published since he made his list that bare inclusion.

<u>Reading List</u>
The Tao Te Ching
The Spiritual Guide of Molinos
The Age of Reason, by Thomas Paine
Zen and the Art of Motorcycle Maintenance,
        by Robert Pirsig
The Golden Bough
The Hathayoga Pradipika
The Bible
Ride the Tiger, Julius Evola
The Crisis of the Modern World, Rene Guenon
Works of Friedrich Nietzsche

Works by William Blake
Works of Joseph Campbell
Works of C.G. Jung
Works of Mircea Eliade
Greek Mythology, Robert Graves
Stranger from a Strange Land, Robert Heinlein
Hamlet and other plays of Shakespeare
The Divine Comedy
Fight Club, Chuck Palhinuik
Egyptian Mythology in general
Norse Mythology in general
Nausea, Jean-Paul Sartre
The Stranger, Albert Camus
The Essays of Ralph Waldo Emerson
Plays of George Bernard Shaw
The Mind of the Middle Ages, by Frederick B. Artz
The Holographic Universe, by Michael Talbot
The Republic, Plato
Walden, Henry D. Thoreau
Poems, Basil Bunting
The Wasteland, T.S. Eliot
The Canterbury Tales, Geoffrey Chaucer
Doctor Faustus, Christopher Marlowe
Paradise Lost, John Milton
Poems by Percy Shelly
Works of Samuel Johnson
Heart of Darkness, Joseph Conrad
Iliad
Ulysses
Oedipus Rex
The Secret Teachings of All Ages, Manly Palmer Hall
The Western Cannon, Harold Bloom
Don Quixote, Miguel De Cervantes
Gulliver's Travels, Jonathan Swift
Faust, Johann Wolfgang von Goethe

Appendix II:
A Brief Index of Historical Figures

Simon Magus (1ˢᵗ Century)

Simon Magus is perhaps one of the greatest
magicians of all time; however he has not been very well
received by history. One of the principle reasons for this is
because of his clash with Jesus' disciples, especially St. Peter.
His was the first recorded instance of a rival religion coming
into conflict with Christianity, and since many of the early
recordings about Simon were from the Church Fathers, it is
understandable that he was given a bad name. He was
known as a Gnostic and a wizard and condemned because
he reportedly tried to buy magical power from one of the
disciples. He is often given credit as the founder of
Gnosticism, but that most likely is not the case. Among
Christian texts he has been called the first heretic.[109]

Simon was a Samaritan from a village called Gitta,
the son of Antonius and Rachel. He studied magic in
Alexandria under a man named John. John was a Jew who
belonged to the sect of Hemero-Baptists. Not much is known
about them. Simon was John's favorite student, but when
John died Simon was absent from the temple, and so a man
named Dositheus was chosen as the new master instead.
When Simon returned, he said nothing about Dositheus
taking the place that was rightly his. However, it did not
take long for tension to arise, principally due to Simon's
superior knowledge. One day Dositheus became angry at
Simon and swung at him with his staff. The stroke swung
clean through Simon and came out the other side of him. All
the while Simon continued to look at this man, perhaps a
slight smile creeping upon his face. Upon seeing this,
Dositheus fell to his knees and swore loyalty to Simon, and

---

[109] Mead, *Simon Magus*, 3-4.

Simon became the new leader. Sadly enough, Dositheus died shortly thereafter.[110]

Many other powers were attributed to Simon by various witnesses. In fact, there are more witnesses to Simon's powers than there were to Jesus'. In the Recognitiones, it is said of Simon that he could:

> dig through mountains, pass through rocks as if they were merely clay, cast himself from a lofty mountain and be borne gently to earth, can break his chains while in prison, and cause the doors to open of their own accord, animate statues and make eye-witness think them men, make trees grow suddenly, pass through fire unhurt, change his face or become double-faced, or turn into a sheep or goat or serpent, make a beard grow upon a boy's chin, fly in the air, become gold, make and unmake kings, have divine worship and honours paid him, order a sickle to go and reap of itself and it reaps ten times as much as an ordinary sickle.[111]

After Peter rejected Simon and his money, Simon shed tears. He took the money and purchased a prostitute named Helen. Simon told his followers that he was the power of God and that Helen was the Holy Spirit, and it was for her that he descended. He explained that she had been trapped in that body and had been reincarnating.[112]

Simon initiated priests and taught them magic. His followers made a statue of Simon after Jupiter and a statue of Helen after Minerva; these they worshipped. Simon collected the blood of females, menstrual blood. He called it "the mysteries of life, and of the most perfect Gnosis." He taught that the world was created through "Dominions and Principalities" which were evil. These beings had various names that had to be learned in order to gain access to the

---

[110] Ibid., 31-32.
[111] Ibid.
[112] Ibid., 11, 25.

148

Appendix II

Universal Father. Furthermore, the Law of Moses was not of God, "but of the left-hand power."[113]

Simon Magus is mentioned in Acts VIII: 9-24 and by quite a few ancient writers such as Justinus Martyr and Irenaeus., and was highly regarded in Rome. Some Romans went so far as to consider him a god. According to Justinus Marytyr a statue was erected of him in the river Tiber and was inscribed *Simon: Deo Sancto*.[114] It was after Simon was honored with a statue that Peter came to Rome to challenge him. As Peter was in Rome and preparing to confront Simon, he told his disciple Clement that their argument was over "certain passages of scripture." Peter then admitted to Clement that there were some outright falsehoods in scripture, but that "it would never do to explain this to the people. These falsehoods have been permitted for certain righteous reasons."

Simon had interesting things to say during his debate with Peter. His biggest issue was that the disciples taught many things that were not true, although he would have acknowledged the truth of some of it. Very little is recorded from this event, and what does remain must be taken with a grain of salt. Among the words spoken by Simon that day during the debate, there have been some fragments that have survived the toil of centuries, and it is from this small sample that we may understand what Simon Magus believed.

As he faced Peter in the courtyard, with the emperor and other noble Romans looking on, his words rang out:

> I say that there are many gods, but one God of all these gods incomprehensible and unknown to all. My belief is that there is a Power of immeasurable and ineffable Light, whose greatness is held to be incomprehensible, a power which the maker of the world even does not know, nor does Moses the lawgiver, nor your master Jesus.[115]

---

[113] Ibid., 10, 26-27.

[114] Text: Corpus Apologetarum Christianorum Saeculi Secundi. Trans. Mead.

[115] Text: Recognitiones II.xxxviii. Trans. Mead.

The emperor was somewhat interested in the debate, but really arranged the meeting because he considered them both to be wizards. He wanted them to fight it out with their magical power like a gladiator duel. According to some sources, Simon Magus summoned a number of demons and began flying around, but Peter fell to his knees and begged God to not allow this to happen. The demons dispersed and Simon Magus fell to his death. So goes one version of the tale.

The version that I prefer is a lesser known one, but one that was recorded in the Clementine literature. Clement was the disciple that had accompanied Peter to Rome. In this tale, Simon used his magic to cause Faustinianus, who was Clement's father, to look exactly like himself. After creating this look-alike, Simon fled Rome. Upon discovering the trick, Peter sent Faustinianus to Antioch, who told everyone of Peter's divine mission. The people there took him to be Simon Magus and so assumed that between the two Peter was the greater, and that Simon had become his disciple as well. At the very least, credit must be given to Peter for his cleverness.

What happened to Simon Magus after he fled Rome? It is difficult to say. Some scholars think that the renowned St. Paul was none other than Simon Magus himself. Although highly speculative, it would help to explain the many disagreements between Peter and Paul. If Simon Magus did not become St. Paul, then it is possible that he returned to Alexandria to lead the Gnostics there, studying and contributing to the now lost Library of Alexandria.

John Dee (1527-1608)

Born in London, Dee was the descendent of an old noble Welsh family. He was quite famous in his time and was known throughout Europe. In his descriptions he was often described as a "mathematician, astrologer and crystal gazer, a fellow of Trinity College." Despite his magical associations for which he is only remembered today, Dee was a respected scientist during his time. He wrote forty-

Appendix II

Appendix II

nine books on scientific subjects and lectured abroad on geometry and astronomy. Queen Elizabeth often consulted him on scientific matters, especially those relating to astronomy and considered him to be her court philosopher, court astrologer and court magician. At the age of 23 he was asked to give lectures on Euclid at the University of Paris. The Russian Emperor offered him a large salary to take up residence at his court, and he received similar offers from Charles V and others. In fact, it was largely through his studies that mathematical research was reborn in England.[116]

Dee was a tireless intellectual and studied a broad range of subjects. During his lifetime he most likely had the largest library in England, and one of the largest in Europe. His ideas, however, were quite out of synch with the trend during this time, which was focused almost completely upon humanism. Dee was a Hermetic Platonist, of the tradition of Ficino rather than Petrarch. During his studies, he became fascinated by astrology, alchemy, the Talmud and the Rosicrucian mysteries. In his diary, he recorded his first sight of the spirit world on May 25th, 1581. A year later, in November of 1582, he saw a bright glow in the west window and then beheld a fabulous being who identified himself as Oriel. He found himself awestruck and couldn't speak. The angel gave to him a piece of crystal by which he might communicate with the beings of the spirit world.[117]

Dee decided to get someone else to do the seeing, while he recorded the visions because it took the entirety of the seer's effort to concentrate upon the crystal. After a short-lived partnership with a man named Barnabas Saul, Dee became acquainted with Edward Kelley. Kelley had some studies in the occult, but is most remembered because he had his ears chopped off for counterfeiting. In any case, John Dee and Edward Kelley proceeded with the visions and the recording of them. Kelley saw a number of beings baring

---

[116] Shepard, *Encyclopedia of Occultism*, 312. French, *John Dee*, 5-6.
[117] Shepard, *Encyclopedia of Occultism*, 312. French, *John Dee*, 22, 43. This crystal is still in existence and until recently was displayed in the British Museum. Since then it has been moved to the Museum of Mankind, located in London.

151

strange inhuman names; some of which claimed to be angelic. They told Kelley a number of things, such as how to find the philosopher's stone and how to properly deal with spirits. Perhaps the most important things that Dee recorded were the angelic hierarchy and the Enochian language.[118] It is for this language that Dee is largely remembered today. There are many today who continue to work with Dee's system and there are several books on the subject, some of which are legitimate. Some of Crowley's greatest efforts were concentrated upon the Enochian system, and he recorded such workings in *The Vision and The Voice.*

Some would say that the enthusiastic Dee was merely duped by Kelley, but there are a number of problems with this view. First, the Enochian language is extremely detailed and complex, yet it is internally perfect, having its own grammar and rules. Also, after the visions, Dee claimed to have found the elixir of life, as per angelic instruction, in the ruins of Glastonbury Abbey. Shortly thereafter Dee began to acquire a great amount of gold.[119]

In 1873, a man named Stainton Moses claimed to have communicated with the spirit of John Dee through automatic writing. Through this writing Moses put forth many details about Dee's life that were later verified by research at the British Museum Library.[120]

Alan Bennett (1872-1923)

(Charles Henry) Allen Bennett was, along with George Cecil Jones, Crowley's primary teacher during his days in the Golden Dawn. Bennett was educated at Hollesly College, and scraped by as an analytical chemist. Bennett was initiated into the G.D. in 1894, taking the motto Iehi Aour, "let there be light." He was always very poor and tormented by illness, but still made a strong impression on other occultists of the time. He was one of the more brilliant minds in the order, and favored mysticism and white magic;

---

[118] Shepard, *Encyclopedia of Occultism,* 313.
[119] Shepard, *Encyclopedia of Occultism,* 313.
[120] Ibid., 316.

he was almost wholly concerned with enlightenment rather than supernatural powers. Bennett had high regard for Mathers, and with him began working on a book of correspondences that Crowley would later expand upon as Liber 777.[121]

Soon after meeting, Crowley invited Bennett to come stay with him, as Bennett was living in a dilapidated shared apartment. Bennett trained Crowley in the basics of magick and tried to instill a devotion to white magick. Bennett was very ascetic and sexually chaste, a marked contrast to Crowley's libertine attitude. Crowley once remarked concerning Bennett's powers: Bennett had constructed a magical wand out of glass, which he carried with him. As it so happened, Crowley and Bennett were walking along one day and came across a group of theosophists who were ridiculing the use of wands. "Allan promptly produced his and blasted one of them. It took fourteen hours to restore the incredulous individual to the use of his mind and his muscles."[122]

In 1900, at the age of 28, Bennett traveled to Asia to relieve his asthma, and to dedicate himself to Buddhism. First he traveled to Ceylon where he studied Hatha Yoga under the yogi Shri Parananda. In 1902 Crowley came to visit him there, and was instructed in Hatha Yoga. During this time both men agreed as to the truth of Buddhism. Later, in Burma, Bennett took the vows of a Buddhist monk, under the name Bhikku Ananda Metteya, "bliss of loving kindness." In 1903 he founded the International Buddhist Society. He later began a periodical called *The Buddhist Review*.[123]

Back in England in 1908, Bennett attempted to spread the study of Buddhism on his native soil, he established the first ever Buddhist Mission in the United Kingdom on 16 July 1908, an event for which the Buddhists

---

[121] Shepard, *Encyclopedia of Occultism*, 140-41. Sutin, *Do What Thou Wilt*, 64.

[122] Sutin, *Do What Thou Wilt*, 65-66.

[123] Shepard, *Encyclopedia of Occultism*, 140-41.

honor him to this day.[124] While in England, he published "The Training of the Mind" in *The Equinox*, Crowley's esoteric publication. Crowley tried to rekindle the friendship that the two had known, but to no avail. By this time Crowley had rejected Buddhism and embraced magick; Bennett had done the exact opposite. He remarked, "No Buddhist would consider it worth while to pass from the crystalline clearness of his own religion to this involved obscurity."[125] It is hard to say what really caused the break between them. Perhaps their visions of the divine really had grown too far apart. It would not be the only dear friend that Crowley would lose.

Some sources say that Bennett intended to travel on to California due to health reasons. But with the outbreak of World War I he found himself stranded, and forced to live in poverty and illness. He died on his native English soil at the age of 51. He wrote two books during his life: *The Wisdom of the Aryes* and *The Religion of Burma*.[126]

George Cecil Jones (1873-1953)

George Cecil Jones was a well-educated man and an analytical chemist by profession. He joined the Golden Dawn in 1895, taking the motto V.N. In 1897, he entered into the second order and took the motto D.D.S. Jones was Crowley's sponsor into the G.D. Crowley often referred to Jones as "The Hermit," and dedicated to him a poem by the same name in *The Winged Beetle*. Jones and Alan Bennett were Crowley's early magical tutors.[127]

Crowley himself describes the meeting in *Confessions*:

> This was a Welshman, named George Cecil Jones. He possessed a fiery but unstable temper, was the son of a suicide, and bore a striking resemblance to many conventional representations of Jesus

---

[124] *Encyclopaedia of Buddhism*
[125] Sutin, *Do What Thou Wilt*, 193.
[126] Shepard, *Encyclopedia of Occultism*, 140-41.
[127] Eshelman, *Mystical & Magical System*, 16.

Christ. His spirit was both ardent and subtle. He
was very widely read in Magick; and, being by
profession an analytical chemist, was able to
investigate the subject in a scientific spirit.[128]
Later, it would be Crowley and Jones who formed the
magical order of the A.A. They continued to work together
through various rituals, and were very close comrades.

Crowley later remarked that Jones "had weakened
in late years. He had married. Life to his optimistic eyes
looked like a green field with a watering trough."[129] Much of
their friendship went downhill revolving a lawsuit.
Apparently, a tabloid called *The Looking Glass* printed an
article about Crowley, and in it hinted that he had a
homosexual relationship with Jones. Jones sued the
magazine for libel. The entire event drew a great amount of
negative publicity upon Jones' head, which he was not in the
least happy about.

For his part, Crowley found the entire situation
hilarious with its idiocy, and was not overly concerned with
it. He was shocked and sad when he received a letter from
Jones telling him that he must take this matter to court and
clear their names or else to break all communications with
him. Crowley refused to do so out of principal or out of
stubbornness and Jones held to his word and ceased
communication.

It is indeed sad that the clamoring of idiots can
destroy a friendship. It is equally sad that it can disrupt the
Great Work. It has been said that after Jones' break with
Crowley, he continued to do a great deal of spiritual work.

Aleister Crowley (1875-1947)
Aleister Crowley is a name that is almost universally
despised by those that know him, although not entirely
fairly. He was hated by other Hermeticists, particularly the
'Hermetic Order of the Golden Dawn,' because of his

---

[128] Crowley, *Confessions*, 172.
[129] Ibid., 759.

libertine ways. He was hated by his contemporary Victorians because his lifestyle was contrary to the morals of the time. He continues to be hated by Kosher Kabbalists today because he intermingled the Kabbala with outside sources, including Taoism, Buddhism, Tantra, Yoga, alchemy, and mythology. This position is particularly interesting considering that the Kabbala can hardly be considered strictly Jewish in any sense. Its entire historical development shows it to be a syncretic work combining elements of Sufism, Gnosticism, Christian asceticism, and Neo-Platonism among other sources. He is hated by most Wiccans for two reasons. Firstly, he was an uncompromising misogynist. Secondly, Gerald Gardner, the founder of Wicca, based all of his magical workings on Crowley's notebooks. The Wiccan creed, "Do what thou will, an it harm none" seems a little too close to Crowley's "Do what thou wilt shall be the whole of the Law."

Although it might seem easy to dismiss Crowley as an "occultist," he was far from the superstitious ignoramus that many paint him to be. It is important to establish this if we are to put faith in Crowley's work and thought. Crowley was an educated man, attended Cambridge University, was an accomplished etymologist. He was a gifted poet, and although perhaps not as well known as some, is included in certain Oxford anthologies to this day. In his writings he demonstrates a deep knowledge of both western and eastern philosophy, and an intimacy with mythology. His style is a hallmark of exquisite modernist prose. Although he failed in his ambitions to be much of a poet, he succeeded in becoming a masterful writer. He was for a time a chess master, beating almost all champions of England and Scotland, but decided it was a waste of time and gave it up. He was also a mountain climber, and succeeded in breaking many records on the peaks of the Himalayas. He studied hermetic magic in England, yoga and Buddhism in the East, and Sufism in Egypt, all in his quest for enlightenment. One of the twentieth-century's greatest unknown geniuses, he was almost universally misunderstood by his contemporaries and continues to be largely misunderstood today.

It has been said that Crowley died insane, broke, and addicted to drugs. A similar argument is often made against Nietzsche. A true seeker cannot let such ad hominem remarks deter from the writings that these men left behind. If indeed they died insane, which is hearsay in any account, then perhaps it is because they put their entire soul and consciousness into their work. I am not being apologetic, which I despise, but merely proving a point. If we cast out those writers who were either had questionable morals, were drug addicted or mentally unstable, then we will have to throw out Hemmingway, Robert E. Howard, Percy Shelly, Lord Byron, William Blake, Stephan King, Friedrich Nietzsche and scores of others.

In the history of mankind, those who do not follow the beaten path are always despised by those of small mind. Blake said that he must either create a system or be enslaved by another man's. Sartre remarked that genius was an attempt to find a way out. The writings of such men are beyond the comprehension of the groundlings, and thus they despise them. In any account, it doesn't really matter. Those that listen to gossip rarely have time in their busy little lives to seek for truth.

Works Cited

Abrams, M.H., et al. eds. "William Blake." *The Norton Anthology of English Literature*. 7th ed. Vol. 2. New York: Norton, 2000. 35-39.

Artz, Frederick B. *The Mind of the Middle Ages: A.D. 200-1500 An Historical Survey*. 3rd rev ed. Chicago: U. of Chicago, 1953.

Barnstone, Willis and Marvin Meyer, ed. *The Gnostic Bible*. Boston: Shambhala, 2003.

Bloom, Harold. *Omens of Millennium: The Gnosis of Angels, Dreams, and Resurrection*. New York: Riverhead, 1996.

Campbell, Joseph. *The Masks of God: Occidental Mythology*. New York: Penguin Compass, 1976.

Crowley, Aleister. *777 and Other Qabalistic Writings of Aleister Crowley*. Ed. Israel Regardie. York Beach, ME: Samuel Weiser, 2000.

---. *The Book of the Law: [Technically called Liber AL Vel Legis sub figura CCXX as delivered by XCIII = 418 to DCLXVI]*. 1938. York Beach, ME: Weiser, 1976.

---. *The Book of Lies*. 1913. York Beach, ME: Weiser, 2000.

---. *The Book of Thoth*. 1944. York Beach, ME: Weiser, 2000.

---. *The Confessions of Aleister Crowley*. Ed. John Symonds and Kenneth Grant. London: Penguin, 1989.

---. *De Arte Magica*. London: Neptune Press, [c. 1914].

---. *Gems from the Equinox: Instructions by Aleister Crowley for his own Magickal Order Selected by Israel Regardie*. Tempe: New Falcon, 1997.

---. *The Gospel According to Saint Bernard Shaw*. Ed. Bill Heidrick. 1953. 6 April 2004. <http://www.hermetic.com/crowley/libers/lib888.txt>.

---. *The Law is for All: The Authorized Popular Commentary on Liber AL vel Legis sub figura CCXX, The Book of the Law*. Ed. Louis Wilkinson and Hymenaeus Beta. Tempe: New Falcon, 1996.

---. *Magick: Liber ABA, Book Four parts I-IV*. 2nd rev. ed. Ed. Hymenaeus Beta. York Beach, ME: Weiser, 2002.

Works Cited

---. *Magick Without Tears*. Ed. Israel Regardie. Tempe: New
    Falcon, 2001.

---. *Thoth Tarot Deck*. Painted by Lady Frieda Harris.
    Stamford, CT: U.S. Game Systems, 1969.

Emerson, Ralph Waldo. *The Portable Emerson*. Ed. Carl Bode
    and Malcom Cowley. New York: Penguin, 1981.

Encyclopaedia of Buddhism. vol. 1 Ed. G. P. Malalasekera et al.
    Colombo: The Government of Ceylon, 1965.

Eshelman, James A. *The Mystical & Magical System of the A. A.*
    Los Angeles: The College of Thelema, 2000.

Fight Club. Dir. David Fincher. Perf. Brad Pitt and Edward
    Norton. Based on novel by Chuck Palahnuk.
    Twentieth Century Fox, 1999.

Fortune, Dion. *The Mystical Qabalah*. York Beach, ME: Samuel
    Weiser, 2000.

French, Peter. *John Dee: The World of an Elizabethan Magus*.
    London: Ark, 1987.

Graham, E.P. "Essenes." *New Advent*. 5 Oct 2003.
    <http://www.newadvent.org/cathen/o5546a.htm>
    .

Gray, William G. *Qabalistic Concepts: Living the Tree*. York
    Beach: ME, 1997.

Holy Bible: Authorized King James Version. Lake Wylie, SC:
    Christian Heritage: 1993.

Kraig, Donald Michael. *Modern Magick: Eleven Lessons in the
    High Magickal Arts*. St. Paul: Llewellyn, 1999.

Mead, G.R.S. *Simon Magus: An Essay on the Founder of
    Simonianism Based on the Ancient Sources with a Re-
    Evaluation of his Philosophy and Teachings*. 1892.
    Chicago: Ares, 1979.

Mill, John Stuart. *On Liberty. The Longman Anthology of British
    Literature*. Ed. David Damrosch. New York:
    Longman, 1999. 1120-1132.

Monnastre, Cris. Introduction. Regardie, *The Golden Dawn*.
    xvii-xxv.

Nietzsche, Friedrich. *Beyond Good & Evil: Prelude to a
    Philosophy of the Future*. 1886. Ed. and Trans. Walter
    Kaufmann. New York: Vintage, 1966.

---. *The Birth of Tragedy.* Trans. Walter Kaufmann. *Criticism: Major Statements.* Ed. Charles Kaplan and William Davis Anderson. Boston: Bedford/St. Martin's, 2000.

---. *The Portable Nietzsche.* Ed. and Trans. Walter Kaufmann. New York: Viking Press, 1954.

---. *The Will to Power.* Ed. and Trans. Walter Kaufmann. New York: Vintage, 1968.

The Norton Shakespeare. Ed. Stephen Greenblatt, et al. New York: Norton, 1997.

Osho. *The Book of Secrets: 112 Keys to the Mystery Within, A Comprehensive Guide to Meditation Techniques described in the Vigyan Bhairav Tantra.* New York: St. Martin's Griffin, 1974.

Pirsig, Robert M. *Zen and the Art of Motorcycle Maintenance: An Inquiry into Values.* New York: Bantam, 1981.

Regardie, Israel. *A Garden of Pomegranates: Skrying on the Tree of Life.* 1932. Ed. Chic Cicero and Sandra Tabatha Cicero. St. Paul: Llewellyn, 2000.

---. "Introduction to the Second Edition Volume I." Introduction. *The Golden Dawn.* 1-6.

---. *The Golden Dawn: A Complete Course in Practical Ceremonial Magick.* 1971. Ed. Carl Llewellyn Weschcke. 6th ed. St. Paul: Llewellyn, 1998.

Scholem, Gershom. *Kabbalah.* New York: Penguin, 1974.

Shepard, Leslie A., ed. *Encyclopedia of Occultism and Parapsychology: A Compendium of Information on the Occult Sciences, Magic [...].* In 3 vol. 2nd ed. Detroit: Gale Research, 1984.

Strong, James. *The New Strong's Exhaustive Concordance of the Bible.* Comfort Print ed. Nashville: Thomas Nelson, 1995.

Sutin, Lawrence. *Do What Thou Wilt: A Life of Aleister Crowley.* New York: St. Martin's, 2000.

Swift, Jonathon. *Gulliver's Travels.* 1735. *The Norton Anthology of English Literature.* Ed. M.H. Abrams, et al. 7th ed. Vol. 1. New York: Norton, 2000. 2331-2473.

Works Cited

Tzu, Lao. *The Way of Life: A New Translation of the Tao Te Ching*. Trans. R.B. Blakney. New York: Mentor-Penguin, 1955.

Westcott, Wm. Wynn. Trans. *Sepher Yetzirah*. 1887. 9 Feb. 2001
    <http://www.hermetic.com/texts/yetzirah.html>.

Printed in the United Kingdom
by Lightning Source UK Ltd.
123916UK00001B/265/A